witnessing 101

witnessing 101

{ **Tim Baker** }

TRANSIT

www.TransitBooks.com

Witnessing 101

Copyright © 2003 by Tim Baker

Published by W Publishing Group, a division of Thomas Nelson, Inc.,
P.O. Box 141000, Nashville, Tennessee 37214.

Cover Design: Riordan Design Group, Toronto, Canada
Page Design: Book and Graphic Design, Nashville, Tennessee

Senior Editor: Kate Etue
Editorial Staff: Bridgett O'Lannerghty and Patty Crowley

Scriptures quoted from *The Holy Bible, New Century Version,* copyright © 1987, 1988, 1991 by Word Publishing, a division of Thomas Nelson, Inc. Used by permission.

Library of Congress Cataloging-in-Publication Data

Baker, Tim, 1965-
    Witnessing 101 / by Tim Baker.
        v. cm.
Contents: Reality check — The truth about truth — The life of Jesus — What the Gospel is — The life of a disciple — Not the Gospel — How to be a friend — Bad ideas — Crafting your story — One person strategy meeting — What to say — What if someone says yes — Failing and freaking out — Long haul evangelism — Living loud — Get it on.
    ISBN 0-8499-4416-3
    1. Witness bearing (Christianity)—Juvenile literature. 2. Teenagers—Religious life. [1. Witness bearing (Christianity) 2. Christian life.] I. Title: Witnessing one hundred one. II. Title: Witnessing one hundred and one. III. Title: Witnessing one o one. IV. Title.
    BV4520 .B26 2003
    248'.5—dc21   2002155418

Printed and bound in the United States of America
03 04 05 06 07 PHX 5 4 3 2 1

For Nicole, Jessica, and Jacob,

You are God's constant reminder that living the
gospel is more important than preaching it.
You are amazing kids. I love being your dad.

Psalm 126:1–3

✦ ✦ ✦

Acknowledgements:

Man. Try writing a book on witnessing. It ain't easy! Many people have worked hard at bringing this book together. Here's who they are, and what they did.

Christina Greenawalt and Jonathan Anderson allowed me to use their stories in chapters thirteen and fifteen. Thanks for letting the world read about you, and thanks for giving this book some heart.

Julie Zielke and Elizabeth Moss, two girls from our youth group, read parts of this book and offered their ideas on how to make it useful. They're responsible for helping reshape this book. Thanks girls!

Kate Etue (and her Transit team) take ordinary words and turn them into extraordinary books. Kate, you are wonderful! Thanks for letting me write for you.

Jacqui Baker (my wife!) read this book with me, edited parts, and allowed me huge blocks of time to write. Thanks for sacrificing your time for this project. You are the most amazing woman I've ever met!

Contents

Introduction

Here's the scene.

You and your best friend just got in line to buy concert tickets. Your mom dropped you off, and you've got to get them and get back to the mall entrance in less than an hour. Looking at the line, this will not be easy. You and your friend begin to pass the time by talking about Stacey, the new girl you saw in the hall yesterday. You think she rocks. Your friend does, too. You begin talking about how you both want to ask her out.

And then it happens.

"Deeeewwwdddd!" Steve walks up. Steve is annoying. You know Steve from church. At church, you tolerate him. Away from church, Steve has the plague.

"Are you guys buying tickets to this concert, too? Man, that is awesome. It's gonna be krunked out! Hey, let's get seats together."

Did I mention that Steve is annoying? Steve gets started, and he just won't stop.

"I've been down with Creed since back in the day. Did I tell you that Scott Stapp and I have the same vision for reaching people for Jesus? Yeah, we're a lot alike. You know what I like to do? I like to take one of their songs, play it over and over for someone I've just met in the park and then ask them if they died tonight, do they know if they'd go to heaven."

You and your friend give each other the Steve-is-a-freak look. Just as the two of you begin to burst out laughing, Steve pulls a portable CD player out of his pocket, gives you a check-this-out look, and heads a few people back.

You watch as he puts headphones on a total stranger and starts the CD. After a few minutes, Steve yanks the headphones off the stranger, opens his Bible, and begins his spiel. The scene is unbelievable. Before long, Steve's project, after trying every other polite tactic, just flat ignores him. Without missing a beat, Steve moves on to the next person.

"Not cool," your friend says.

"What a freak," you respond.

Okay. So maybe you've never actually been in that situation. You've never been present when a believing friend laid out his or her faith in the hopes of rescuing someone. Do you know a Steve? Ever been a Steve?

Have you ever tried to tell someone what you believe about Jesus and been laughed at? Ever tried and got the whole thing totally messed up? Ever felt like you *ought* to tell someone about Christ but were too scared, didn't know what to say, or were totally not sure about how to go about it?

Look. You are not alone. The truth is that loads of believers want to tell others about Christ but are too scared. Many try but don't know what to say. So, if you're scared or unsure, you are not in a crowd by yourself.

When you look at what Jesus said to do with Him, His reality, and His truth, you can't ignore that you've *got* to say something about Him to unbelieving friends. So, what do you say? How do you live? And how do you even know that what you've said or how you've lived has made a difference?

There are no easy answers. And, anyone who tells you that there's a simple formula for saving your friends probably doesn't know *your* friends.

As you try to share what you believe about Jesus, what *isn't* cool? It isn't cool to be a Steve. And it *is* cool to be yourself. If God has done something wonderful in you, then it's totally cool to be yourself, and tell others what He's done in you in a way that's both *comfortable* (that fits you) and *compelling* (that helps the other person understand Jesus and the change He's made in you).

Witnessing 101 will help you be both comfortable and compelling. Look, we won't load you down with unimportant, useless stuff that might confuse you. You're not going to get a silly system that will help you put notches in your Bible. Instead, you'll find simple stuff you can use as you try to live out what you believe around your unbelieving friends.

chapter one

Reality Check

It's really easy to totally mess up something really great and embarrass yourself. Many years ago Al Capone, a ruthless gangster, ruled the city of Chicago. He didn't stop at anything to make money in underhanded or dishonest ways. He was known for running alcohol into Chicago when the city was under prohibition. FBI agent Elliot Ness was assigned to handle the problem of Al Capone. It was his job to take Capone down at any cost. Ness assembled the best lawmen around him, and he set out to break apart Capone's network of corruption.

One of Ness's first attempts at pulling Capone's network apart was the night he went after one of Capone's warehouses. The attack plan was simple: Wait until it was late at night, attack Capone's warehouse, break open the cases of illegal alcohol, get good press, become known as the guy who successfully attacked Capone (which might possibly scare or anger Capone), and keep after it to eventually beat Capone.

Well, the night of the big raid had come. Acting on a tip they'd received, Ness had assembled a group of men and charged them with the task of raiding Capone's warehouse. Ness had his men hiding outside the warehouse—guns drawn, hearts pounding, and Ness standing with them, ready for a huge success. At the signal, the men rushed the warehouse. They kicked in doors, broke open shipping crates, and discovered a shipment of umbrellas.

Can you imagine the embarrassment of Ness and the rest of the police as the headlines spread throughout the city? They must have looked really ridiculous. Setting out to uncover illegal alcohol only to uncover very legal umbrellas.

It's very easy to jump to conclusions, to think we've got ourselves together, and then step out and make total fools of ourselves.

Witnessing can be like that. We think we're ready . . . we step out to tell our friends about Christ and end up making ourselves look silly. Or we come really close to telling someone about Jesus but at the last minute chicken out and feel totally stupid. It's easy to get caught up in a method of sharing Jesus that we think will work but just doesn't, or a way of sharing Jesus that is incorrect. When we do that, we can cause some serious damage.

Telling your friends about Jesus is more than just spewing out all the truth you've been taught since you were three or all the stuff your youth pastor taught you about God. It's more than being able to answer your friends' questions, and it's more than just being able to defend your beliefs.

Sharing Jesus with our friends can be more difficult than we imagine. And because it involves so many different elements, we take some crazy steps to make the whole thing seem simple. It's as if we leave important things out or overemphasize a bunch of "steps" that are easy to use, just so we can encourage more people to share their faith. When we do this, we end up with an incorrect picture of what witnessing really is. The following five statements sum up the ways we try to change witnessing and in the end ruin it!

1. God needs your help!

It's easy to get the whole witnessing thing wrong and to think that we're a major part in the transaction between an unsaved person and God. The truth is that God is more powerful than we think. Who created the world? Who created you? Who sent His Son to die? God did all of those things. If He was able to do that, does He really need *us* to tell others about Him?

Look, God has everything under His control. Did you get that? EVERYTHING. That means that He has you, your best friend, your parents, and the people on the other side of the world all taken care of. If He's God, and He can create the world, He can easily change the hearts of everyone on the earth at once if He wants to. He doesn't *have* to use us to tell others about Christ; He *chooses* to.

2. God doesn't need your help!

This one is very closely related to the first, but it's important enough to make a distinction. While God doesn't *have* to use us to tell others about Christ, He *chooses* to use us. Why? Because the gospel is best presented within a relationship. God chooses to use us because our friends can see our relationship with Jesus, and that helps them understand.

The really cool thing about this is that God *wants* to use us. Because He's God, He can use whatever means He wants to when bringing others into a relationship with Him. Even with all of the power that He has, we're simply His hands and feet in the lives of our friends. We know the truth, and God gives us strategic opportunities to tell our friends the truth.

3. You have to know everything.

One of the biggest reasons we don't tell others about Christ is our feeling that we've got to have all of the facts about the whole thing straight. We think it's important to have our speech right, to have all of our passages memorized, and to know how to close the deal.

Actually, this isn't true. Okay, it's kind of true. It is true that we need to know what we're talking about, and we need to know and understand what the Bible says about important issues. But it's incorrect to think we have to be a walking Bible dictionary, to get caught up in making sure that we have *everything* straight before we go and tell someone about Christ. Sometimes it's okay to be honest with people and tell them you don't have an answer—then go with them to find the truth.

{ For help knowing what to say, check out chapter 11 }

4. You've got to have a thrilling testimony.

Ever heard someone who has had a really tough past share his or her testimony? Man, it can be really exciting. They get up to the microphone and begin the story . . .

"Before I met Jesus I was a mass murderer, I sinned in all kinds of nasty ways, and I was even mean to puppies . . ."

When you hear those kinds of testimonies, don't you begin to think, *Dude, nothing like that has ever happened to me. I'm just gonna stay outta the way of this person and let them tell people about Jesus. I'll go and do something else for God.*

Yeah, I know how that feels. If you don't feel your testimony is the best, it's easy to want to just shut up and let someone with an engaging, fantastic story take over. Look, you don't need a fantastic story about how Christ has changed your life. You don't need to lie to make it more

{ **Need help with your testimony? See chapter 9** }

interesting, and you don't need to hide yourself and never tell anyone. God has given you a testimony even if you've never done anything wrong in a real public way. You can still testify to how God has led you to Him. He's constantly creating a new story in you as you're following Him. You don't need to have sinned big-time to make God interesting to someone searching for Him.

5. God's keeping score.

God's love doesn't increase as you introduce more people to Him. It's not like He's keeping track or making notches on a gold brick in heaven. Do you have friends who have some uncanny ability to share Christ with others and are always telling you about their "conquests"? Know someone who tells you that God wants you to reach as many people for Him as you can and will remember all of your "saves" when you get to heaven?

While God *has* engaged us in the process of helping others know Him, He *doesn't* call us to out-do our best friends. It's not like God wants us to try to save more people than anyone else, and it's certainly not fair to say that God wants to see how many people we'll save for Him. It's not a raffle, and the prize doesn't go to the person God uses to save the most souls. God wants us to tell others about Him in a noncompetitive, loving way.

What Is God Paying Attention To?

It'd be unfair to lay out all of the things that God *didn't* like or thought were ridiculous without explaining the things that God *is* looking for. If God doesn't need those five things, then what things does God want from us? Here are a few ideas:

I. God is looking for our willingness.

If you know Jesus (and if you're reading this book, chances are that you do) then hopefully you'll realize that God's not interested in perfection as we share Jesus. Yeah, He wants us to do our best, but He's not expecting us to have things perfect. He's after our willingness. He wants us to want to tell others about Him.

Willingness is completely different for each of us. For some, that willingness translates into an unending and very outward passion where we go and tell everyone we meet about Him. For others, willingness means a quiet determination to drop truths about God into the minds of unbelievers. Willingness doesn't mean we all share Jesus the same way with the same intensity. We've just got to be willing and allow God to take our hearts, minds, and bodies and do something amazing with them.

2. God is looking for our readiness.

The Bible makes it very clear in many places that we're to be prepared to tell others about Jesus. It's not enough to be willing;

we've got to be prepared, too. (But don't use "lack of preparation" as an excuse not to share the good news of Christ with someone!)

Preparation comes in all kinds of ways. We need to spend time in God's Word and do our best to know it. We've got to know our own salvation story well enough to share it with others. We've got to know how to handle possible objections and even some of the tough intellectual concepts about God. Most of all, our preparation ought to be directed by God. We ought to allow Him to arm us through His Holy Spirit and bring us to the place where we're ready, by His power, to tell others about Him.

3. God wants us to try.

The effort to attempt to tell others about Jesus is possibly the toughest part of sharing God's Word. We can be willing, and we can even prepare ourselves, but actually doing it can really scare us!

Why is the act of witnessing so difficult? Beyond feeling unprepared, lots of us are just flat afraid. We're worried about what our friends will say or what they'll think of us. We're worried that they'll ignore us or choose not to accept Christ. We're afraid of failing, and we're scared that we'll say the wrong thing. I think that God honors our attempts in ways we could never understand. He honors

{ For encouragement as you tell your friends, see chapter 16 }

our attempts with someone saying *yes* to Christ, and He honors our attempts by just planting a seed in the person we're talking to. Often, we don't know what effect our words have had on our friends, but God is watching. He's watering the seed we plant, and He'll keep working on it.

In order to encourage people to witness, we've really distorted the Gospel, and we've messed up by creating things that are unneccessary. How do we get around those broken, useless humanly created rules? We follow God's original intentions. We need to be willing. We need to be ready. And we need to try.

So, you've got to ask yourself . . . why? Why the heck do we need to say anything to anyone? After all, God is powerful, and it's not like we could really ever make someone decide for God. So what's the big deal?

Consider this. Consider, what if you didn't say anything to anyone about what you believe about God? What if you never attempted a conversation? What if you never brought the subject up with a close friend? What if you choose not to tell anyone about the change that's happened in your life?

What if You Don't Tell Your Friends?

Choosing not to tell people about Christ actually does have eternal implications. It's a weird but true fact that our lack of effort could affect the eternity of our friends. Need an explanation of the problem unsaved people face? Here's the rundown of humanity's future without knowing about the gospel.

Created in God's Image

Genesis 1:26–27 makes the origin of humanity easy to grasp. How did humans begin walking the earth? Genesis points out that humanity—men and women—were created in God's image. In some way

{ For help working this into a talk with a friend, see pp 107–109 }

we look like God, act like God, think like God, and are emotionally built like God. Our purpose is to have fellowship with God.

Fell Apart over Fruit

In the Garden of Eden, Adam and Eve had all their needs met. They were in perfect union with God. But these first two humans chose to disobey God's command to not eat the fruit from the Tree of the Knowledge of Good and Evil (Genesis 2:17). Eve ate first, and then Adam ate . . . all because the serpent in the garden convinced Eve that what God said wasn't really what He meant. Genesis 3:1–13 paints all of this for us:

> Now the snake was the most clever of all the wild animals the LORD God had made. One day the snake said to the woman, "Did God really say that you must not eat fruit from any tree in the garden?"
>
> The woman answered the snake, "We may eat fruit from the trees in the garden. But God told us, 'You must not eat fruit from the tree that is in the middle of the garden. You must not even touch it, or you will die.'"
>
> But the snake said to the woman, "You will not die. God knows that if you eat the fruit from that tree, you will learn about good and evil and you will be like God!"
>
> The woman saw that the tree was beautiful, that its fruit was good to eat, and that it would make her wise. So she took some of its fruit and ate it. She also gave some of the fruit to her husband, and he ate it.
>
> Then, it was as if their eyes were opened. They realized they were naked, so they sewed fig leaves together and made something to cover themselves.
>
> Then they heard the LORD God walking in the garden during the cool part of the day, and the man and his wife hid from the LORD God among the trees in the garden. But the LORD God called to the man and said, "Where are you?"

> The man answered, "I heard you walking in the garden, and I was afraid because I was naked, so I hid."
>
> God asked, "Who told you that you were naked? Did you eat fruit from the tree from which I commanded you not to eat?"
>
> The man said, "You gave this woman to me and she gave me fruit from the tree, so I ate it."
>
> Then the LORD God said to the woman, "How could you have done such a thing?"
>
> She answered, "The snake tricked me, so I ate the fruit."

The result of Adam and Eve's sin rippled into their relationship with God and continues to ripple out into the world today. Theologians describe the results of Adam and Eve's sin in the following ways:

Inherited sin. Because of what Adam and Eve did, their sin affected the entire scope of humanity. Their sin has been passed down for the entire existence of humanity. This is often called our "sinful nature." We have a constant bent toward sin.

Committed sin. Because we have a constant inclination toward sin, we commit sins every day. We fall because of decisions we make and things we choose to do that are outside of God's will.

God Instituted Sacrifices to Have Fellowship with Us

Before the Fall, Adam and Eve had a close relationship with God. After the Fall, that relationship was ruined. In fact, God describes how much the God-Man relationship was ruined and what the effects of the Fall were on humanity in a post-Fall speech in Genesis 3:14–19. Women would have pain in childbirth; men would labor over the ground. Both Adam and Eve were expelled from the Garden of Eden.

Because Adam, Eve, and (as a result of the Fall) the rest of humanity were separated from God after the Fall, God reached back into the world and set up a system of sacrifice. Why? Through the blood of animals and other offerings, humankind is able to reestablish a relationship with God and receive forgiveness for their sins.

Ever wondered what kind of sacrifice humanity had to offer to God before Jesus came? Look, the list is long and kind of sick, so go check out Leviticus 3–7 and you'll see the different kinds of sacrifices and the results each sacrifice had on the life of the worshiper.

Jesus Came as the Ultimate Sacrifice and the Only Way to Heaven.

Way back in the Old Testament, before the sacrificial system and before the Ten Commandments, there's a hint about Jesus. God gave Adam and Eve a speech just after they fell and told them how He'd conquer sin, Satan, and death. In Genesis 3:15, God promises that Eve's offspring would crush the head of Satan.

> *I will make you and the woman*
> *enemies to each other.*
> *Your descendants and her descendants*
> *will be enemies.*
> *One of her descendants will crush your head,*
> *and you will bite his heel.*

Many biblical scholars agree that this is a prophecy about Jesus totally conquering Satan and the results of the Fall. They say that Eve's descendants' crushing the serpent's head translates into a deadly strike on Satan's head at some point in history. They go on to conclude that the bruise to the heel implies a minor strike to Jesus, something that He'd easily recover from (like being crucified and put in a tomb).

He's prophesied all throughout the Old Testament, and in the New Testament Jesus proclaims in John 14:6 that He is the only way to heaven: "Jesus answered, 'I am the way, and the truth, and the life. The only way to the Father is through me.'" Through the next few chapters, we'll discover the importance of Jesus and how His death opened the door for all of humanity to have a direct relationship with God.

Reality Check

God doesn't have a set way for you to share Jesus with your friends. He wants you to use your unique strengths to tell others about your relationship with Him. He just wants you to do it. Without Him, your unsaved friends will face an eternity separated from God. With Him, your friends have the opportunity to live forever in an amazing relationship with their Creator. God is counting on you to be an honest and connected friend so your friends can see the reality of the Savior and their need for Him.

chapter two

The Truth about Truth

Here's a little experiment. Take a few minutes and try this out.

First, go and get something from your room. It doesn't matter what the object is, just go and get anything. Now, stand at the door, facing into your room and walk forward to the left until you're in the corner. Drop the object. Next, walk *backward* to where you started.

Now, look at where you placed the object. From where you're standing, you've placed the object in the left corner of your room, right? Okay, here's where the experiment begins.

Turn around. Now answer the following question: Where is the object located in the room?

If you answered that question with *in the front left corner of the room*, you're wrong. Since your back is now facing the object, it is located in the back right corner of the room. Your perspective has changed. The object never moved—you did.

Truth is often viewed this same way. While truth doesn't change, people look at what is true and offer their perspectives on it. In the discussion we often lose sight of the fact that truth never really changed or moved. It stayed the same. What changed is the different viewpoints of what truth is.

Why You Need to Know This

A chapter like this is, well . . . it's boring. Who wants to read page after page of philosophy and theology—probably no one normal! But think about it for a second. If everyone in the world today looks at truth differently, then it's up to Christians to help set things straight. And since we're taking the gospel to a world that easily dismisses our belief as "their truth, not ours," we have to be as prepared as we can be.

We can't just approach people with the truth of Scripture without being prepared with both biblical truth and a basic understanding of some general philosophical concepts that help explain and defend our truth—*the* truth.

As believers, we define truth based on two distinct categories. First, there's the truth that we hold as believers that comes from Scripture. In other words, everything we believe about God, sin, etc. is gleaned from God's Word. Second, we discover what truth is by using our minds. We can think philosophically about God, eternity, sin, or whatever. These two ways to approach and understand truth are really cool. God has given us proof and explanation from His Word and from solid thinking, and all of it leads us to a deeper understanding of what truth is.

Let's attack the issue of truth—first from the perspective of Scripture and then using a little philosophy.

Truth and the Bible

You've got to ask yourself: If the Bible is almost two thousand years old, how can we be sure that it is actually true? How can the Bible be accurate when so many people have been involved with its development? There were all kinds of writers who put their effort into it. There were loads of translators who took the original documents and copied them so others could read God's Word. During our lifetime people have reproduced God's Word into new and different translations. This makes it easy for some to look at the Bible as a book directed by humans rather than by God.

When we say that God's Word is true, we mean that it is just flat true. Nothing in it is untrue. Why is it true? Because it is from God's mouth. Where do you go in Scripture to get that? Second Timothy 3:16–17 lays out our basic understanding of Scripture:

> *All Scripture is given by God and is useful for teaching, for showing people what is wrong in their lives, for correcting faults, and for teaching how to live right. Using the Scriptures, the person who serves God will be capable, having all that is needed to do every good work.*

1. Scripture Is God-Given

This God-given concept is often referred to as *inspiration*. God inspired the writers to put into words the message He had for the original audience. This same God who breathed these words into the minds of the writers has walked with His word through years and years of translation efforts. As people have translated Scripture, God has kept it without error. This idea is often called *inerrancy*.

2. Useful For . . .

The idea that believers can "use" God's word is a mind-blowing concept. The God-given document that contains God's truth is useful in the life of all believers to guide them in their walk with Him. This is often referred to as *illumination*. Through the Holy Spirit, God's Word is powerful in the life of believers today.

What Truths Do We Get from the Bible?

1. Our Concept of God

Revelation. We know about God and His character through two types of revelation: general and special. Very simply, general revelation is God making Himself known through the created order of the universe. Just like a painting bears the brush strokes of the painter, creation bears the hand of its Creator—God. In Romans 1:19–20, Paul almost yells this out as he describes how God is revealed through His creation.

> *Yes, God has shown himself to them. There are things about him that people cannot see—his eternal power and all the things that make him God. But since the beginning of the world those things have been easy to understand by what God has made. So people have no excuse for the bad things they do.*

The other side of revelation is an idea called special revelation. Special revelation is God proving Himself and His existence through the miraculous. What kinds of things fall into this category? Jesus' miracles are considered special revelation. So are those awesome moments in the Old Testament where God bent natural laws and did something supernatural within His creation. Examples of this are God holding the sun still (Joshua 10:12–14) and using Elisha in an interesting moment with an ax head (2 Kings 6:1–7).

2. General Attributes of God

The Bible reveals all kinds of things about God's personality. In fact, Scripture is dripping with explanations about God's character. There are too many for us to check out here in this chapter, so I'll just list them and tell you where you can find them in Scripture. Look them up when you get the chance.

General Attributes:
- Leviticus 11:44—God is holy.
- 1 Samuel 2:2–8—God is sovereign: He is the final authority and ruler over everything.
- Job 42:2—God is omnipotent: He can do anything He wants.
- Psalm 90:2—God is eternal.
- Psalm 102:25–27—God does not change.
- Psalm 139:7–11—God is omnipresent: He's everywhere, all the time.
- Psalm 139:15–16—God is omniscient: He knows all things actual and potential.
- John 5:26—God is self-existent.

3. Attributes That Affect Us

These attributes are slightly different because they directly affect us. When we say that God is eternal, that's all good, but His immortality doesn't necessarily affect us. However, these attributes are superobvious in our lives.

- Numbers 14:18; Psalm 103:8—God is patient.
- Psalm 19:9—God is just.
- Romans 2:4—God is kind.
- Ephesians 2:7–9—God is grace, and He offers that grace to us.
- James 5:11—God is mercy.
- 2 Peter 3:9, 15—God is patient.
- 1 John 4:8—God is love.

However, it's important to realize that though God has made Himself known through His creation and Scripture, we can't know *everything* about God. God is at the same time knowable and unknowable. He's awesomely mysterious. So it's cool to be able to explain who God is, but it's not cool to take what we've studied about God's nature and think that we've got Him all figured out.

How We Handle Truth, Scripture, and the Existence of God

The apostle Paul was the master at grasping truth and presenting it in ways that people could understand. Acts 17:16-34 paints a picture of Paul debating the skilled philosophers of Athens. These guys may or may not have known Paul, but that didn't keep him from presenting truth to these philosophers. And the way Paul presented truth was extremely skilled. Acts 17:28-31 demonstrates Paul's skill:

"We live in him. We walk in him. We are in him." Some of your own poets have said: "For we are his children." Since we are God's children, you must not think that God is like something that people imagine or make from gold, silver, or rock. In the past, people did not understand God, and he ignored this. But now, God tells all people in the world to change their hearts and lives. God has set a day that he will judge all the world with fairness, by the man he chose long ago. And God has proved this to everyone by raising that man from the dead!

We live in Him. We walk in Him. We are in Him. This is Paul quoting the ancient poet Epimenides who lived about 600 B.C. This poet would have been well-known to the people sitting around listening to Paul.

We are His children. Paul is quoting the poet Aratus who lived from 315 to 240 B.C. Again, a well-known poet in Paul's time.

The cool thing that Paul is doing in this moment is using the truth about God and infusing it with the thinking of the time. Paul's speech demonstrates three essential things believers must do with truth.

1. Paul understood truth. He wasn't afraid to interact with it. He wasn't afraid to challenge truth, or have his ideas about what was true challenged.

2. Paul knew fairly current thinking. While the philosophers were using thoughts and ideas from long ago, they were discussing and applying them in their current day. Paul knew their foundational beliefs.

3. Paul had thought through his idea of truth, was prepared to explain it in a way the thinking men of his time could understand.

Notice too that Paul used their truth to help explain the truth about God.

If Paul had not completely thought through all of these, he would have never been able to discuss truth with these guys, and he'd have never been able to effectively tell them about God.

These days, if we want to be effective with unbelievers, we have to be able to discuss truth—both the truth of Scripture and the truth about God that's philosophical in nature. How do we do that?

- *Know what you believe.* In this book, we've given you the basic understanding of sin and salvation. Take some time to expand your understanding of what "truth" is. You can do this by using an Internet search engine, typing in the word *truth* and reading some of the pages you get. Or, you can ask your pastor for some books that have helped him understand the concept of truth.
- *Know current thinking about God, truth, religion, etc.* Again, an easy thing to do by surfing the Net. But, you can also get a grasp of these ideas from watching television, or reading some magazines that talk about what's happening in the world. Above all, the easiest place to learn about current thinking is to listen to what your unsaved friends are talking about.

Paul's example is totally clear. Truth is too important to ignore. Current truth is too important to pass off as "ungodly" or sinful. We have to know what we believe, and infuse it into current thinking so our friends will completely understand what we're trying to say, and why we live the way we do.

After looking at truth, and the way Paul presented it, you've go to ask "How did Jesus handle truth?" Since he was the Truth, wouldn't studying Jesus present us with the best example of how to tell people the truth? Yep. Jesus was the master at presenting the truth. Let's look at how Jesus helped people understand the truth.

chapter three

The Life of Jesus

Imagine:

- being so passionate about your friend's health that you go donate blood for a major operation she's got coming up.
- being so concerned about your parents' stress level that you mow the lawn without them asking.
- being so worried about your brother that you buy him lunch and just sit and listen to him talk about how his life is going.
- being so happy about your best friend's new job waiting tables that you go there for dinner, even though you can't stand the restaurant.

Sacrifice seems impossible for many of us. Sacrifice takes

time and effort. As humans we've got this natural instinct that says, *Go after your own interests first . . . help your friend tomorrow!*

But for Jesus, sacrifice was second nature. While people around Him were self-serving, He was constantly sacrificing. While He was preparing to die for humanity, His friends were arguing about who would get to sit next to Him in heaven. As He served, people were confused. As He was beaten, crowds of people cheered. As He was being crucified, soldiers divided up His clothes. He constantly confused people close to Him—not because He wanted to be confusing, but because He did things so selflessly that most people couldn't comprehend it.

This man, who is both God and human, who died for us, and who is our good news, also led us in how we ought to tell others about Him. Imagine that! Jesus was both the Good News and the best trainer in how to share the good news. People often talk about the way Jesus told stories to communicate truth, but Jesus was also the master at communicating truth in other ways. How did He do it? Let's look at four examples from His life.

Jesus and Nicodemus: The Art of Conversation

You probably memorized John 3:16 when you were little. But did you ever consider that that verse is a part of a conversation between two rulers? One a ruler of the church on earth, the other the ruler of the world. Check out John 3:1–21 and see what a strange conversation this really is:

> *There was a man named Nicodemus who was one of the Pharisees and an important Jewish leader. One night Nicodemus came to Jesus and said, "Teacher, we know you are a teacher*

sent from God, because no one can do the miracles you do unless God is with him."

Jesus answered, "I tell you the truth, unless one is born again, he cannot be in God's kingdom."

Nicodemus said, "But if a person is already old, how can he be born again? He cannot enter his mother's body again. So how can a person be born a second time?"

But Jesus answered, "I tell you the truth, unless one is born from water and the Spirit, he cannot enter God's kingdom. Human life comes from human parents, but spiritual life comes from the Spirit. Don't be surprised when I tell you, 'You must all be born again.' The wind blows where it wants to and you hear the sound of it, but you don't know where the wind comes from or where it is going. It is the same with every person who is born from the Spirit."

Nicodemus asked, "How can this happen?"

Jesus said, "You are an important teacher in Israel, and you don't understand these things? I tell you the truth, we talk about what we know, and we tell about what we have seen, but you don't accept what we tell you. I have told you about things here on earth, and you do not believe me. So you will not believe me if I tell you about things of heaven. The only one who has ever gone up to heaven is the One who came down from heaven—the Son of Man.

"Just as Moses lifted up the snake in the desert, the Son of Man must also be lifted up. So that everyone who believes can have eternal life in him.

"God loved the world so much that he gave his one and only Son so that whoever believes in him may not be lost, but have eternal life. God did not send his Son into the world to judge the *world guilty, but to save the world through him. People who believe in God's Son are not judged guilty. Those who do not believe have already been judged guilty, because they have not believed in God's one and only Son. They are judged by this fact: The Light has come into the world, but they did not want light. They wanted darkness, because they were doing evil things. All who do evil hate the light and will not come to the light, because it will show all the evil things they do. But those who follow the true way come to the light, and it shows that the things they do were done through God."*

Imagine the contrast in worlds between Jesus, the Savior of the world, and Nicodemus, one of the major religious leaders of his time. See, the problem was that the religious leaders (Nicodemus included) didn't recognize Jesus as the Messiah, but still knew He was someone interesting.

Do we know what Nicodemus thought about Jesus? Well, we know two things for sure. First, we know what he thought of Jesus by the way he addressed Him. He called Him *Rabbi,* which means "teacher." Jesus had obviously gained respect as a teacher, and Nicodemus recognized that. Some people think that Nicodemus might have been speaking tongue-in-cheek and was only calling Jesus a teacher out of a fake kind of reverence. I don't think so. Nicodemus might not have understood Jesus' teachings or understood who Jesus *really* was, but he probably respected Him as a good teacher.

Second, we know what he thought of Jesus because he approached Jesus at night. There might be two reasons for this: avoiding the crowds that would have been around Jesus or not wanting his friends to see that he was talking to Jesus. After all, a religious leader's speaking to Jesus would have been seen as equal to his agreeing with Him. But whatever the reason, Nicodemus took a risk to talk with Jesus. Jesus honored his risky behavior with an excellent example of how to discuss truth. Here are the highlights:

1. *Jesus led Nicodemus into a deeper understanding of the born-again idea.* He didn't hit him with the huge concepts of who He was until later in the passage. At first, Jesus just began by a simple leading response to Nicodemus's question.

2. *Jesus willingly engaged in a conversation with Nicodemus.* It's true, most of the stuff in this passage is Jesus talking, but it's in conversational language. Jesus isn't preaching; He's talking . . . discussing . . . and it reads casually. That's the key element in this passage—the whole conversation thing. Jesus masterfully took Nicodemus to a place he never thought he'd go and with a person he never thought he'd have a chance to talk with.

Jesus and the Rich Guy: The Art of Honesty

Mark 10:17–23 demonstrates Jesus' unparalleled ability to be honest. While on His way to a certain town, Jesus encountered a very rich young man. The guy knew who Jesus was and called Him a good teacher. Then the guy opened a can of worms and without knowing it got at the heart of one of Jesus' main themes while He was on earth—the struggle between riches and personal holiness. The man's question is basic, probably honest, and very eye-opening.

He asked, "What must I do to inherit eternal life?"

Jesus, being the Master at answering those kinds of questions, responded to the guy with, "Go, sell everything you have, give it to the poor, and then follow me."

Here's what's really cool about what Jesus said: First, it's obvious that Jesus knew just how rich this man was. Probably not a big stretch, since the man was probably dressed very well. Jesus got at the heart of where this guy's trust was.

Second, Jesus knew just how much this man loved his stuff. Jesus might have said, "Sell everything but one hundred horses, give almost all of it to the poor, then follow me." Nah, Jesus' response to the man showed He was extremely aware of exactly where this man placed his trust.

Third, Jesus challenged this man's commitment to his religion. In their conversation, the man made it clear that he knew Jewish teachings. In fact, most historians believe that this man was probably a very good Jew. In the Jewish religion at the time, almsgiving (giving to the poor) was a very popular way to show how religious you were. Jesus' statement about giving everything that he had to the poor challenged his commitment to his religion.

But what's key in this passage is Jesus' honesty. He didn't mix words; He didn't soften the truth so the guy could handle it. He was just flat honest.

Jesus and the Samaritan Woman: The Art of Compassion

Check out John 4:1–26. There's so much going on in this story that you've got to really get behind a lot of history to understand Jesus' compassion.

The Pharisees heard that Jesus was making and baptizing more
followers than John, although Jesus himself did not baptize

people, but his followers did. Jesus knew that the Pharisees had heard about him, so he left Judea and went back to Galilee. But on the way he had to go through the country of Samaria.

In Samaria Jesus came to the town called Sychar, which is near the field Jacob gave to his son Joseph. Jacob's well was there. Jesus was tired from his long trip, so he sat down beside the well. It was about twelve o'clock noon. When a Samaritan woman came to the well to get some water, Jesus said to her, "Please give me a drink." (This happened while Jesus' followers were in town buying some food.)

The woman said, "I am surprised that you ask me for a drink, since you are a Jewish man and I am a Samaritan woman." (Jewish people are not friends with Samaritans.)

Jesus said, "If you only knew the free gift of God and who it is that is asking you for water, you would have asked him, and he would have given you living water."

The woman said, "Sir, where will you get this living water? The well is very deep, and you have nothing to get water with. Are you greater than Jacob, our father, who gave us this well and drank from it himself along with his sons and flocks?"

Jesus answered, "Everyone who drinks this water will be thirsty again, but whoever drinks the water I give will never be thirsty. The water I give will become a spring of water gushing up inside that person, giving eternal life."

The woman said to him, "Sir, give me this water so I will never be thirsty again and will not have to come back here to get more water."

Jesus told her, "Go get your husband and come back here."

The woman answered, "I have no husband."

Jesus said to her, "You are right to say you have no husband.

Really you have had five husbands, and the man you live with now is not your husband. You told the truth."

The woman said, "Sir, I can see that you are a prophet. Our ancestors worshiped on this mountain, but you Jews say that Jerusalem is the place where people must worship."

Jesus said, "Believe me, woman. The time is coming when neither in Jerusalem nor on this mountain will you actually worship the Father. You Samaritans worship something you don't understand. We understand what we worship, because salvation comes from the Jews. The time is coming when the true worshipers will worship the Father in spirit and truth, and that time is here already. You see, the Father too is actively seeking such people to worship him. God is spirit, and those who worship him must worship in spirit and truth.

The woman said, "I know that the Messiah is coming." (Messiah is the One called Christ.) "When the Messiah comes, he will explain everything to us."

Then Jesus said, "I am he—I, the one talking to you."

For starters, Jews and Samaritans didn't get along. In fact, they hated each other. It goes way back in history to when the Jews had land that the Samaritans wanted. They ended up fighting over it, and there'd been bad blood ever since. Most of the problem is described in 2 Kings 17, and you can read the story there if you want the details. Anyway, it's enough to say at this point that Jews and Samaritans were enemies. Culturally, Jesus would have been expected to completely ignore this woman or be extremely rude to her. He didn't do either.

Second, Jesus is God, and God can't stand adultery. He hates it. And this woman was adultery in the flesh. Her life was consumed with it. Jesus knew that and pointed it out to her. But Jesus didn't sit and discuss it with her. He didn't attempt to point out how wrong it is. She knew she was sinning, and it was enough for Jesus to point it out.

That's two strikes against her: She was a Samaritan; she was an adulterer. No doubt Jesus could wail on her. But He didn't.

Notice in this passage the way Jesus drew her into discovering who He was without being condemning. Jesus knew that her lifestyle totally clashed with God's truth, but He didn't hammer her with rules and laws. He basically just loved her with His words. That's Jesus demonstrating compassion. Because He was a Jew, He could have been hateful toward her. Because she was deeply adulterous, He could have been condemning. He didn't do either, and in the end He won the woman over.

Jesus and the Disciples: The Art of Service

It's crunch time. A few days before He was led away to be killed, Jesus met with His disciples one last time. The plan? Simple: Eat a meal. Pray. Hang out. Then go to Gethsemane for prayer. Simple plan. Really, even with that plan no one knew what was going to happen except Jesus. He knew the complexity of the evening. He knew what was coming.

There, in the Upper Room with the disciples, Jesus demonstrated the art of service. The disciples were probably expecting Him to say all kinds of important things. They were expecting Jesus to give them final teachings about God or heaven. And they were certainly (because they'd been waiting for this one for a while now) expecting Jesus to be transformed from the suffering, persecuted Messiah to the conquering King who would prove

Himself to the authorities and wipe out the opposing religious hypocrites. Instead, Jesus took an approach that totally caught them off guard. He got a basin of water and a towel, and he washed His disciples' feet.

This was an especially dirty task. Back then everyone wore sandals, and the streets were not paved. Add that up and you've got dirty, stinky feet. Isn't that an unbelievable picture to get in your mind? Dirty feet and Jesus (the Creator, the Savior) kneeling like a servant to clean them. Cleaning off the very stuff He used to make those feet.

The disciples didn't need convincing. They didn't need winning over. Jesus was demonstrating the kind of people He expected them to be. It's as if Jesus was saying, "Okay, boys. You know what to say. You know how to say it. So, now I'll show you how to live it."

Jesus did and gave the disciples the gift of service and the challenge to live it like an art form.

Imitating Jesus' Style

Jesus was the master at having a good conversation, being honest, being compassionate and serving. We're not God, so we can't do things exactly the way Jesus did them. But we can learn what He did and imitate Jesus' style in these four areas when it comes to sharing our faith. Here's how.

The Art of Conversation

When I was a kid it was enough just to have all the facts lined up when it came to God. All you were expected to do when you told someone about Jesus was to give them your carefully memorized testimony in a crafty sales pitch. No joke. It was okay just to nail someone with the gospel. After all, if they rejected it, it was totally their fault.

These days if you approach someone with a set of facts and a heavy-handed delivery, you can do a lot of damage. You can turn them off to the gospel. You can offend them. The trick is getting started. It can be tough to know how to get a conversation started with a nonbeliever. Take a moment to think through how you might start a conversation with someone who doesn't know Christ.

Write down three different ways to begin a conversation with someone who's not a believer:

1. _____

2. _____

3. _____

The real way to get people thinking about spiritual issues is to model Jesus' ability to use conversation. And to do that, you've got to lead conversations the way Jesus did. Look at Jesus' conversation with Nicodemus. What can we take from that and apply to our witnessing ability?

Be casual. Jesus' ability to have a conversation was powered by His casual approach. He was not trying to jam truth into Nicodemus; He was just talking. He was willing to discuss. He was not threatened by Nicodemus's questions. Instead, He was inspired by them. Listening to Nicodemus, Jesus got a picture of what Nicodemus was really after.

Listen. Jesus listened to people like no one else did. It's no wonder sinners were attracted to Him! He was probably the only religious leader who would listen to them. His ability to have a conversation with Nicodemus was fueled by his ability to listen.

Practice. You'll never be casual in your ability to talk to your unsaved friends unless you practice. And listening . . . really listening, takes practice. Do you ever listen to someone and at the same time think about the next witty comment you're going to make? Ever listen just to be polite or just long enough so you can politely excuse yourself when they're finished talking? Jesus doesn't listen like this. You shouldn't either.

The Art of Honesty

Let's say that one day your best friend comes over and you decide to start talking about religion. The two of you have been tight for forever, since you were kids. Anyway, you're talking, and she begins telling you about the stuff she's been doing with her new boyfriend. (The two of you hardly ever see each other anymore since she's been dating him. You'd *love* to talk with her about that, but you don't have the guts.) As you're talking about him, she tells you that he's been going to her church with her, but in turn, she's been going to church with him. To his church . . . which is a well-known cult. She tells you that even though she doesn't agree with everything his church believes, she's decided to start going with him regularly because she really likes him and wants to be with him all of the time.

In your head, you're going nuts. Your best friend is about to join a cult, and she's sitting there telling you about it. You've got two choices. You can (a) shut up to preserve your friendship, or (b) be honest by telling her what she's doing is wrong (and possibly lose your friendship with her). What do you need to do? You need to be honest. Can you do that? Maybe? Maybe not?

Honesty is key in helping people get to know Christ. But being honest isn't easy for all of us. Some people see the risks of honesty and choose to just be silent. What prevents you from being honest with your friends?

Write down three things that prevent you from being honest with people:

1. _____

2. _____

3. _____

Jesus' ability to be compassionately honest was unbelievable. He never mixed words, and He always told people the truth. If you're going to imitate Jesus' honesty, you've got to be honest at all times. Period.

That means, if you see your friends doing something that will hurt them, you've got to risk the friendship and tell them the truth. If they're lost, don't know Christ, and are without hope, it's up to you to be honest with them about Jesus so that they can know the happiness that you know.

The Art of Compassion

Compassion is a tricky word. Not because it's difficult to do, but because so often we feel that if we're compassionate toward someone who's living in sin we're approving the way they live.

For example, one day you're eating at a fast-food place with some of your friends. As you get to your favorite booth, a smelly, dirty, kinda' scary-looking man walks up to you and sheds a long tear-filled sob story about how he's been homeless for three weeks and hasn't eaten in two days. At first you don't believe him, but the more he goes on the more believable his story gets and the more you want to help. When the guy finally finishes his speil, you're crying, he's crying, and you're reaching for your wallet. You give him everything you have. You invite the guy to eat with you and your friends. He declines, and you watch him walk over to the gas station next-door and buy cigarettes and a beer with the money you just gave him.

That experience might keep you from ever wanting to give money again. But we don't need a bad experience to keep us from being compassionate. Often it's just the fear of commitment or insecurity that keeps us from reaching out to others with compassion.

Take a second and think through some of the things that prevent you from being compassionate.

Write down three things that prevent you from being compassionate toward people:

1. _____

2. _____

3. _____

How did Jesus show compassion? He sat and listened, and He didn't sacrifice honesty. He just listened, told the truth, and acted with love. Imitating Jesus' compassion isn't as difficult as we think. How do we do it? Love people. Listen. And let God work His compassion through us.

The Art of Service

This one might be the toughest. It's easy to talk about Jesus. It's even easy to live some of the things that He told us to live. But when it comes to actually serving people, many of us have a difficult time with that. It's probably because serving others takes a lot of time. We want to serve our friends, but because it takes so much time we'd rather just ignore what Jesus did. But Jesus didn't serve the disciples just because He felt like it. He served them because He wanted them to imitate Him. How do we imitate Him? We look for opportunities. Got ideas?

Write a few ways you can serve your unsaved friends below:

- _____

- _____

- _____

- _____

- _____

- _____

- _____

- _____

- _____

Getting It All Together

Jesus was honest. He told the truth. He served like no other religious leader did or has done since. He was the Master of conversation and knew exactly what to say and when to say it. Jesus was the ultimate person of compassion. He let truth speak for itself. And when He spoke, He was controlled, kind, and loving.

We can do what Jesus did. You can do it. While we can't be Jesus (we're not God, we're not the Savior), we can act and live like Him. We can be totally compassionate or completely honest. And remember—Jesus combined these qualities. He was never only compassionate or only honest. He was compassionately honest. He was honest in His service. These qualities that He had were always combined in an effective way to reach people. As we're attempting to imitate the Master Communicator, we need to be willing to combine these qualities, just like Jesus did.

Our goal is to help our friends know Christ. The best way to do that is to imitate the Master communicator. At all times. In all situations.

chapter four

What the Gospel Is

Take this test . . . see how you do.

You're standing in line to get tickets for the new hot movie that just hit the theaters. You've been there for a while (lots of people want to see it), and you're really feeling impatient. In front of you, there are two girls arguing about their churches.

The first girl says something like, "Yeah, well. We don't do anything like that. Really, we just do our own thinking—we have dinners and stuff like that. If people want to come, that's cool. But if people don't want to come, it's okay, too."

The other girl is on the warpath. She says back, "But, what about people who need to come to your church? I mean, what if you're the only hope that some people ever have, and coming to one of your church dinners was the only way they'd hear about the gospel?"

The other girl comes back with a, "Look. My church just doesn't do that. The gospel? Really. Look. God loves everyone. And the truth is, everyone gets to go to some kind of heaven."

So you're there, and you've been listening, and you've been to enough youth group stuff to know that something in that conversation isn't right. What would you say? Imagine that you're there, and you've got the guts to break into the conversation. What would you say?

_____

_____

_____

_____

_____

_____

_____

What's the big deal?

Well, what we're after is a deep understanding of the gospel. What it is, what it does, and why it's important. After all, when you're giving someone the gospel, what are you giving them? The truth! Here's the truth you're communicating:

First, the gospel is rooted in God, Jesus, and the Holy Spirit. The word *gospel* literally means "good news." When you share the gospel, you're sharing the good news with them.

What's the good news? The good news is found in Scripture. There are two important places you need to go to really get a grip on the gospel. They're both in the gospel of John.

> *In the beginning there was the Word. The Word was with God, and the Word was God. He was with God in the beginning. All things were made by him, and nothing was made without him. In him there was life, and that life was the light of all people. The Light shines in the darkness, and the darkness has not over-powered it.*
>
> *There was a man named John who was sent by God. He came to tell people the truth about the Light so that through him all people could hear about the Light and believe. John was not the Light, but he came to tell people the truth about the Light. The true Light that gives light to all was coming into the world!*
>
> *The Word was in the world, and the world was made by him, but the world did not know him. He came to the world that was his own, but his own people did not accept him. But to all who did accept him and believe in him he gave the right to become children of God. They did not become his children in any human way—by any human parents or human desire. They were born of God.*
>
> *The Word became a human and lived among us. We saw his glory—the glory that belongs to the only Son of the Father— and he was full of grace and truth.* (John 1:1–14)

You could read that passage all day and make endless lists of all the important ideas in it. But these verses clearly explain what the gospel is.

The Word was with God, and the Word was God. The Word here (and you've got to go to the original language on this one—

the Greek!) originally was *logos*. In this passage, *the Word* is refer-
ring to Jesus. So the passage can read "In the beginning was
Jesus . . . Jesus was with God, and Jesus was God." Cool, huh?
Wait, it gets better.

The idea of *word* here carries an Old Testament meaning, too.
The word of God in the Old Testament was a really special one.
When Moses went up on a mountain and heard from God, he
brought back important, life-giving words from God. Those
words gathered people together. The Israelites would get together
to hear from God. God's word was what brought people together.

John might be making a point here by calling Jesus the
Word. He might be saying that Jesus was the great uniter. As He
lived and walked the earth, Jesus brought more people into fellowship with God than could have been imagined.

The Word lived among us. Jesus (the Word) made his dwelling
among us. *Dwelling* literally means "tented." In other words, God
lived in heaven, saw how lost we were, and decided to leave His
home in heaven and live—tent—among us. Amazing! So if the
first chapter of John tells us *what* happened, the third chapter
tells us *why*.

> God loved the world so much that he gave his one and only Son
> so that whoever believes in him may not be lost, but have eter-
> nal life. (John 3:16)

Setting: Jesus is in a semiheated discussion during a well-
known, well-respected conversation with a man named Nicodemus.
Nicodemus was a Pharisee, so it was pretty amazing that he'd be
talking with Jesus in the first place.

God loved. Imagine for a moment the most unconditional,

pure, honest, nondysfunctional love there could possibly be. Got it? Good, that's God's love. How does the Bible describe it? When it speaks of God's love for you, it mostly uses the word *agape*. Agape love is unconditional. It's the kind of love that's not sexual, but it's more than friendship. So God loves you enough to do amazing, tough things for you. Read on through this verse; see what God did.

The world. The world came from somewhere. Scientists, philosophers, and theologians all agree that the world formed somehow. The problem is getting them all to agree how. The English use of the word *world* here is ineffective at conveying what John was saying. The actual word means "the entire cosmos," not just planet Earth—the entire universe.

He sent His Son. You've got to ask, "What does it mean that God sent His Son?" First, it means that the Son was willing to go. The Trinity is a weird thing to try and pick apart because the three people in it (the Father, the Son, and the Holy Spirit) are definitely one person. They are three different personalities of the Godhead. But the Bible describes these beings in three very different ways. Second, it's important to note that the concept of God's love is clearly tied to His sending His Son to make a way for these mixed-up people to spend eternity with Him.

To die. Note: John 3:16 doesn't say that Jesus died. Actually, it just says that God sent His Son. But the implied idea (and we know what Jesus came to do, since we can look back in history) is that Jesus was sent to die.

Jesus wasn't put in an electric chair, and He wasn't drugged to death. He was killed in an extremely violent way. How? Here's a quick rundown:

- He was beaten. Several times Jesus was kicked, spit on, and hit.
- He was scourged. Jesus received thirty-nine hits with a leather whip embedded with animal teeth and bones. Each time Jesus was whipped, the whip ripped hunks of flesh, fat, and muscle off His body.
- He was robed and unrobed. This doesn't sound bad, right? Well, the process of putting a robe on Him and then ripping it off would reopen the wounds He had received from His scourging, causing more pain and more blood loss.
- He had nails driven through His wrists and feet. Okay, this is obvious. It had to hurt.
- He was nailed to a cross, hung upright. The pain of being nailed on the ground was bad, but when He was placed upright, the weight of His body pulling against the nails in His hands and feet would have been awful. More pain. More blood loss. His body rubbed against the cross, reopening the wounds on His back. His arms pulled His ribcage making breathing very difficult.
- He had a spear driven through His side. Halfway through the crucifixion, a soldier drove a spear through Jesus' side, attempting to speed up Jesus' death.

When we say, "Jesus died for me," it's almost like we forget the pain, agony, and sacrifice Jesus endured for us. But when you really break it apart, it's easy to see how much devotion went into it. Jesus didn't just meander up to a gas chamber, sit down, and drift off to heaven. Nope. His death was violent, humiliating, and extremely painful.

The Truth of the Gospel

What does all of that boil down to? Simple: Jesus came to die for all humanity so the way to God could be open for anyone who believed in Jesus. Simple and complex. On one level, the gospel is easy to grasp. Jesus' death, opening the way to God is the ultimate awesome moment. And on another level, it's totally impossible to understand.

Want to discover how to grasp and live this truth? There's no better group to study than the first disciples. Looking at them will help us understand how we're supposed to live out the truth of the gospel. These men lived God's love in amazing ways. And understanding how they lived will push us to live out this awesome gospel.

chapter five

The Life of a Disciple

Peter and Andrew had been raised fishermen, just like their
fathers before them. They had fishing in their blood. These were
rough men—the kind you'd likely find at a bar on a Friday night
or that would get into a fight pretty quickly.

Every so often, these rough men would stand at the edge of
the ocean and just look at it. Can't you imagine how they must
have wondered what they'd haul in the next day? Can't you hear
their conversations? What do you suppose they talked about as
they sat in their boats and headed out to bring in their nets?
These were rough men. That's why Jesus' call to them one day as
He was walking the shore was so strange.

Jesus, walking on the shore of the Sea of Galilee, noticed
these men working. And here's the strange thing: Remember
who Jesus is? He's God. He has all the power of the entire universe

under His control. He can change men's minds without any effort. He can change the consistency of water without trying. And this God (the only One) can choose anyone He wants to use to change the world.

Just for a second, imagine that you're a leader and you can choose anyone you want to work for your cause. You can enlist the power of any person in the world. Who would you choose? Bill Gates? Oprah? Bono? Julia Roberts? Or some guys down on the dock unloading fish?

Here's what Jesus did. He called these rough, hard working, unruly fishermen, and He did it with two simple words: "Follow me."

Kind of anticlimactic, huh? You'd think that Jesus, even though He chose tough guys, would at least have a more inspiring speech, right? Possibly He'd have thought it out more. No, that's not Jesus' style. He's simple. He's straightforward. And He knows who to pick to get the job done.

We know He chose the right guys by their response to His ascension. Fast forward from the moment Jesus called the disciples to the time He left them and went into heaven (just after His resurrection). Acts leads us into an awesome understanding of how the disciples lived after Jesus went to heaven.

Acts 1:6–11. Here's the scene: Jesus has just risen from the dead, and He's spent His time hanging with the disciples. He's been walking with them, eating with them, and spending some time getting a few last-minute things straight with them before He goes away. After Jesus said everything that He needed to, He began to rise. He floated higher and higher until the disciples couldn't see Him anymore.

So there they were. All alone. Just the disciples, the promise of the Holy Spirit, and that's about it. The disciples without Jesus probably felt like a band without their lead singer. You'd think that would have been it.

But that *wasn't* it. The disciples didn't quit, and they didn't give up. A few days later, they were all together, both the disciples and a large crowd.

Acts 2:1–41. While they were together, a sound like a roar fell on them. They were filled with the Holy Spirit. This is where the fun began!

With the power of the Holy Spirit and the experiences they had with Jesus, the disciples were ready to go and tell others about their experience. What did these bold men do? This passage in Acts gives us a huge amount of information.

Peter gives the message of a lifetime. Jews had come to Jerusalem from all over—as far as Rome, which was about eight hundred miles away. They were there for Pentecost. And Peter, full of the Holy Spirit and the power of God, got up and preached about Jesus. Over three thousand people came to Christ that day.

Acts 3:1–4:22. Next, Peter and another disciple were walking through Jerusalem and they came upon a man begging at the city gate. The guy couldn't walk. All Peter had to do was talk to him, tell him that he was healed, and he was healed. That miracle is amazing, but so is what Peter did when he was confronted by the ruling religious body of the time.

Annas and his family (who were also the religious leaders) wanted Peter to answer for what he'd done. Actually, Annas was just doing his job. He was responsible for checking on all of the religious people of the time, especially the traveling preachers, to make sure they were not teaching heresy. Annas wanted Peter to explain why the miracles happened.

Peter did, saying he acted through God's power, which frustrated Annas even more. So Annas and his friends got together in a private session and tried to decide what to do with Peter and his message. They came back to Peter with a "please be quiet" request. They didn't plan to hurt him, as long as he stopped preaching about Christ. Peter's response was simple and straightforward: "We can't help it. We have to talk about what we've experienced."

It's already obvious what Peter and the disciples did. Let's break it apart for just a moment.

1. The disciples told people about the love of God.

It's interesting to read the messages these people gave in Acts. While the places they preached were different, the heart of their messages were the same. Their honesty came face to face with the religious hypocrisy of the time. They reminded religious leaders that they were the people who killed Jesus. And they always remained confident. More than anything, they simply told people about their expereiences with Jesus, what he had done in their lives . . . and they reminded everyone of God's unending love.

2. The disciples demonstrated the love of God.

Remember, these early disciples actually knew Jesus. Their experiences with Him weren't things they lived through after just a week with Jesus. They spent a lot of time with Him. They were well aware of the love of God. And because of that, these men knew what it meant to live the love of God. They knew what it meant to love people as only Jesus could. Their service exemplified God's love. Their confidence and lack of fear demonstrated how sure they were of it.

3. The disciples trusted Christ.

Imagine spending time with Jesus. Then imagine Him being killed and you feeling lost and alone without Him. After following Christ, the disciples were left alone to live *for* Him *without* Him! The only option was total trust in God. Left on their own, they chose to follow Christ. They also chose to do what He commanded.

4. The disciples were very, very human.

It'd be easy to look at these guys and get a superhuman view of who they were. After all . . . these men walked with God. They knew every teaching Jesus preached (although they often didn't understand the real meaning behind what He was saying). They were witnesses to Jesus' unbelievable miracles. Not only that, Jesus gave them the power to do exactly what He did. So when these guys went out to do the ministry—to tell people about Jesus—they experienced many of the miraculous things that Jesus did.

But even with all of the awesome things that these guys did, they were remarkably human. They smelled. They were sometimes in bad moods. They cried and laughed. They fought with each other. Okay, so Scripture doesn't record *all* of the bad moments of the disciples, but it does record some. These men who were so close to Jesus were at the same time very close to their human nature. But even though they were human, their humanness didn't get in the way of their ministry.

Are We Disciples?

We could look over Scripture, see what the disciples did, know that they had firsthand knowledge of Jesus, and say to ourselves,

"Dude. Those were the disciples, and that isn't me. If you want me to do something for Christ, then fine. But I'm not any *disciple*." It's easy to say that we're not as powerful, empowered, gifted, skilled, or prepared as the first twelve who followed Jesus were.

What Does Scripture Say?

Does the Bible actually say we are disciples? Are we the same kind of disciples with the same kind of power? Yeah, it does. Yeah, we are.

Jesus makes it clear that the first twelve disciples weren't the only disciples Jesus was counting on. Check out John 13:34–35.

> *I give you a new command: Love each other. You must love each other as I have loved you. All people will know that you are my followers if you love each other.*

Later on in Scripture, as Jesus is about to ascend into heaven, He makes the infamous statement to the disciples: "So go and make followers of all people in the world" (Matthew 28:19).

We're told that the first disciples were called upon to make disciples of others. And, Jesus notes that a significant mark of the life of a disciple is love. How does all of that add up? As modern-day disciples, we're called to imitate what Jesus did and what the disciples were able to do. We're called to love others. Love is the mark of the disciple. It's the deciding factor between people who *call* themselves disciples and those who *are* disciples.

My Life As a Disciple

You're a disciple.

Now that you know and understand that, let's talk about what that means today, in our century, at your age. With all of your skills and abilities, strengths and weaknesses, God has called you to the wonderful adventure of being His representative on earth. Let's get our minds around what that really means. Take some time to fill out these basic questions.

1. In what ways have you followed Jesus?

_____

_____

_____

_____

_____

_____

2. In what ways have you failed in your walk with Christ?

_____

_____

_____

_____

_____

3. What major spiritual mountains have you climbed?

_____

_____

_____

_____

_____

4. How have you loved others?

_____

_____

_____

_____

_____

Take a look at your life as Jesus' disciple. Look over the last two pages and review your walk with Him. Later on, in chapter 9, we'll use some of these thoughts to build your walk into your testimony.

One More Disciplelike Aspect

These first believers imitated Jesus. They lived love just like the Savior. They did everything within their power to follow in Jesus' footsteps. We've discovered that they sometimes had amazing mess-ups, and they often had some hefty successes.

One thing we haven't mentioned is that these guys faced all kinds of anti-Jesus beliefs. In Jesus' time there were all kinds of religions and offshoots of the Jewish belief system. And after Jesus left the earth and turned things over to the disciples, more and more beliefs popped up that claimed to possess the ultimate truth. This made the disciples' jobs much more difficult. While they had to tell others about Jesus, they also had to set many people straight on what the truth really was. They had to know what the gospel was, and they had to know what other beliefs of the time were preaching in order to actively speak against the massive amount of untruths that were flying around.

These days it's no different. While Christianity continues to spread, so do false religions, false beliefs, and inaccurate truths. As you seek to live like a disciple and follow in the footsteps of Jesus, you'll no doubt encounter incorrect beliefs. You've got to be ready to face these if you're going to be effective. So check out the next chapter and see what the gospel is *not*.

chapter six

Not the Gospel

If you want an interesting experience, go to a computer, fire up an Internet search engine, and type in any of the following words: *God*, *Christianity*, *religion*, or *Jesus*. Any of those words will return a strange variety of Web pages. There are pages that help people out of what they call the "mind control of Christianity." There are alternative religions that attempt to prove that God does not exist. There are all kinds of pages aimed at disproving Christianity. There are also loads of pages that preach an alternative kind of gospel, one built on what the Bible says, but stretched or twisted in such a way that it sounds true but really isn't.

These days, there are all kinds of weird beliefs about God, Jesus, faith, and all the other major cornerstones of Christianity. There are so many that it'd be impossible to answer all of their silliness in this book. But there are general themes and some major twists that are important to know.

Why? Because as you launch out to tell others about the change that happened to you, people will be more than happy to tell you what they believe. Keep your eye out for these ideas, and use the Scriptures provided to find out what the Bible says is true about some of these major issues.

Lies about God

The earth is God. It's easy to get confused about the God/earth debate. God is in everything, right? So He's in the earth, right? So the earth is part of God, right? Not really. Scripture is very clear that the earth is a created thing. Check out Genesis 1 for the origin of the earth.

God's love changes. Because we make mistakes, people often think that God stops loving us until we ask forgiveness. God does not stop loving us when we sin. It's not possible to make God so mad that He stops loving you. Jeremiah 31:3, John 3:16, and Romans 5:8 are some places you can go to find out the truth of God's love.

There are many gods. World religions have made their way into the mainstream and have confused the picture of God. Many non-Christian religions preach that there are additional gods who are equal with the God of the Bible. This isn't true. Exodus 20:2–4, Deuteronomy 6:4, and Romans 1:21–25 clear up this question.

There are many paths to God. Because God can seem massive and mysterious, lots of people feel that there are many paths to

God (meaning that Jesus, Mohammed, Buddha, and others were all correct in the way they get you to God). This isn't true. Matthew 7:13–14 and John 14:6 point out the correct and only way to God: Jesus.

You are a god/goddess waiting to happen. Some major religions preach that because God lives in you, you are actually God. And the sooner you realize that you're able to approach godlike status, the happier you'll be. Actually, God does live inside Christians, but that doesn't mean that they're divine. Genesis 2:7, Romans 8:23, and Ephesians 1:5 help us understand that we're human and not divine.

God created the world, then left it alone to run itself. This is often called Deism, and it's an incorrect way to look at God's involvement in the world and in our lives. God created the world and has always been actively and intimately involved in it. Genesis 1–3, Acts 17:24–28, and 2 Corinthians 5:17–19 record God's active involvement in the world.

Lies about Jesus

Jesus is a created being. Some religions teach that Jesus was created sometime before God created the world. Others teach that Jesus was created later in history, specifically to serve as a once-for-all sacrifice for lost humanity. Jesus is actually a lightning rod for all kinds of wacky beliefs, and it's impossible to describe all of them. So to get an accurate understanding of who Jesus is, check out these verses: Psalm 102:25, John 1:1–18, Hebrews 1:10, and Hebrews 13:8.

Lies about Heaven

There's more than one heaven. Some religions teach that heaven is a variety of planets, and when you die you go live on one of the planets. This isn't true, and here's where you can go to discover what Scripture says about heaven: John 14:1–4 and 2 Corinthians 5:1–10.

Heaven is open to anyone who's good. Some people believe that anyone who is good gets to go to heaven. The Bible teaches against this and tells us that heaven is only open to people who have a personal relationship with Jesus. You'll find answers to this in Luke 13:1–5, John 14:5–6, Romans 10:9–10, and 1 John 1:7–9, 4:15.

Lies about Sin

Some sins are worse than others. Everyone's trying to run from sin these days, but that's not to say that they're trying to stop sinning. They're trying to remove the stigma of sin and create a new doctrine that preaches that there are some sins that are less wrong than others. Does the Bible agree with this? No. Here's where it speaks clearly about sin: John 8:34, Romans 6:23, Romans 14:23, 1 Corinthians 15:56, and James 1:15.

Lies about Satan

Satan and Jesus are brothers. Some pseudo-Christian religions come close to effectively explaining a fictitious relationship between Jesus and Satan, and they say that they're brothers.

Jesus and Satan aren't brothers, and the Bible is very clear about this in 2 Corinthians 11:14 and 2 Peter 2:4.

Satan and God are equal. Some religions speak of God having an equal counterpart that's just as powerful as He is. They say that God's counterpart is as evil as God is good. They believe that this balance of power explains evil in our society. This is a bogus idea, and the Bible explains Satan's place in God's kingdom in Isaiah 14:12–15 and Matthew 4:10.

Lies about Salvation

Salvation is the result of our effort. Many Christians believe that we have some part in the process of salvation. While it is true that we have to confess our sins, the act of salvation is totally up to God. We sometimes believe that we can earn God's favor or gain salvation through our own effort. The Bible speaks loudly against this in Romans 6:23, Ephesians 2:8, and 1 John 4:15.

Another sacrifice will do. Understanding the barrier between God and man can be difficult to comprehend, and it can feel tough for some people to surrender themselves and accept Jesus. Because of these feelings, people often think up creative ways to get around the sacrifice Jesus paid on the cross. They'll either think up another kind of sacrifice or deny what Jesus did and try and ignore the necessity of who Jesus is. However, the Bible says that Jesus' sacrifice on the cross is the only sacrifice that restores the God-human relationship. Where do you find this in the Bible? Check out: Matthew 7:13–14, John 14:6, and Ephesians 1:6–8.

Lies about Humans

You are a product of evolution. You are a machine. The naturalist worldview preaches that humans are soulless machines that are better governed by rewards than by God's will. Are we really just machines that are just evolved beings? No. Genesis 1:26–27, Psalm 139:13, and Jeremiah 1:5 tell us about our origin.

You are basically a good person. We want to think that all of humanity is really, really good and that everyone is, at the very center of their beings, a very good person. The Bible says that this is not true and helps us understand our fallen nature in Psalm 51:1–5 and Romans 3:10–18.

chapter seven

How to Be a Friend

Close your eyes (after you read this paragraph!). Think about your ideal best friend. What is s/he like? What does s/he do for fun? How does s/he treat you? How often do you hang out?

Take a moment and describe the world's best friend:

_____

_____

_____

_____

_____

_____

_____

_____

Describe a time when someone was a really good friend to you. What made him or her a good friend?

_____

_____

_____

_____

_____

_____

_____

On the lines below, write a definition of what friendship is:

_____

_____

_____

_____

_____

_____

Friendship is a tough word to define. It's easy to say you're friends with someone, but it's often tough to follow through and actually be a friend.

What the Bible Says about Friendship

One of the major words used in the Bible for friendship is the Greek word *philos*. This word is linked to the whole idea in Greek society of friendship as a selfless, loving relationship between two people. But the overwhelming idea in the New Testament that surrounds the concept of friendship is "the sharing of experiences." In other words, in the minds of the people who wrote the Bible, friendship was built, established, and deepened as people lived life together.

Philos is tied closely to another popular word for friendship often referred to as *agape*. *Agape* is selfless and self-giving love, like God's love for us. Humans can also express an agape kind of love—especially for close friends, parents, spouses, and siblings. Agape love is a total giving of yourself to another person.

Agape and *philos* are two awesome words that help us understand what friendship is. But Jesus adds some ideas that show what *real* friendship is.

The Biblical Definition Goes Further . . . Jesus Explains It All

What does Jesus say about friendship? He wraps up the concept of shared experiences and selfless love in a statement He made one day to His disciples.

This is my command: Love each other as I have loved you. The

*greatest love a person can show is to die for his friends. You are
my friends if you do what I command you.* (John 15:12–14)

Check out the ideas that Jesus tells us about friendship in
that passage:

- Love equals laying down your life.
- We are encouraged to give up our lives for our friends.
- The love we have for our friends must mirror the kind of
  love Jesus expressed to His friends.

In this short statement, Jesus helps us understand the broader
concept of friendship and the kind of friendship that God expects
us to exemplify toward our friends. It's a kind of combination of
philos and agape, with a total giving of yourself. And all for the
sake of your friends.

How do you live this out in the real world? How are you supposed to live selflessly, sharing experiences and possibly laying
down your life for your friends? And all for the sake of the gospel?

Two men who lived through the September 11 tragedy in
America helped us understand the selflessness Jesus is calling us
to live. On that day America learned what real friendship is, as
we also learned what terrorism in the twenty-first century is.

After first tower was hit, people trapped on the top floors of
the World Trade Center did their best to get out however they
could. One man, hopelessly trapped on one of the top floors, began
to make his way to the bottom. He attempted many staircases,
trying desperately to get out of the building. Every staircase he
tried was blocked either by debris or smoke too thick to breathe.

Finally he found a staircase that appeared passable and began to make his way down. After only a few flights of stairs, the walls began to buckle, falling in, and he became trapped between floors. Immediately he began to yell. Unfortunately there was almost no one around to hear his cries for help.

About the same time, another man leading a group of people down a parallel staircase thought he heard something on the other side of the wall. Having worked in the building for a long time, he knew that there was a staircase there. As he attempted to yell through the wall to the trapped man, there was another crack and another buckle. The building was shifting. A hole was created just big enough for the trapped man to yell through, pleading for his life. The leader worked to create a larger hole, and the trapped man slowly wedged his body through and traveled with the group out of the building to safety.

Can you see the parallels to us sharing Christ with others?

The leader was present. Had he not been in the stairwell, the trapped man would have had no hope. (If Christians aren't willing to befriend non-Christians they have no hope.) The leader worked selflessly. Without regard for his own safety, he led the group in rescuing the trapped man. (We must be diligent, going to any lengths to share the good news.) The leader led the rescued man out of the building. It wasn't enough to just rescue the trapped man. The trapped man had to be led out. (You can't just share the gospel and run, you have to develop a relationship for discipleship—just like Jesus and his followers.)

We Have to Be Present

We struggle with this so often. On the one hand, we want to be present with our nonbelieving friends. Because we love them, or because we're concerned with how they're living, we want to live life with them and actually be present with them. But on the other hand, we feel that if we're there with them we're condoning what they do, how they live, or what they believe. We feel that if we actually do try to befriend them, others will look at us and think that we're just as "sinful" as our friend is.

Look, you're not alone. Most believers have struggled with this. If you are trying to figure it out today, here are a few ideas to consider.

First, you're actually not approving of your friends' actions by hanging out with them. Actually, if you hang out with nonbelieving friends, you're living just like Christ did. If you open the Gospels to almost any passage, you'll notice that Jesus hung out with sinners all the time. He was known as the friend of sinners. As He spent time with the sinners of His day, He never compromised His beliefs—He never sinned! Jesus was here to rescue sinners. He couldn't have rescued any sinner if He hadn't spent time with them. The same goes for us. If we're called to tell our friends about Jesus, how can we do that without hanging out with them? We can't ignore them; we have to go where they go and be present as they live their lives. If we don't hang out with them then all we are to our friends are people who had some kind of a life change then ignored them. That's not what Jesus has called us to do.

On the lines below, name a few unsaved friends and the things they do or the places they go that might be difficult for you.

1. _____

_____

2. _____

_____

_____

3. _____

_____

_____

4. _____

_____

_____

5. _____

_____

_____

We Have to Work Selflessly

Trying to live selflessly can feel like you're trying to pull nails out of wood with your teeth. It's not part of our fabric to deny ourselves and seek others' health, safety, and success. What are some key elements to the idea of selflessness?

Surrender. The best way to think of this word is in a really negative way. For example: Some guys have held up a bank. All of the hostages inside are terrified. The bank president is worried about his fortune; the tellers are concerned about not ever seeing their children again; the customers are fearing for their lives. The police arrive. What do they say to the robbers? Yeah, you already know. They probably say, "Surrender! Put your hands in the air!" In order to surrender, the thieves have to give up their plans, risk jail, and live under a new set of rules.

Self-surrender isn't much different from that. When we give up ourselves for a friend, we have to give up our plans and all of the things that we think are important for us. We have to risk everything and give ourselves over to God to allow Him to set out new plans for us.

Risk. Selflessness involves risk. It's the same kind of risk that's involved in bungee jumping or skydiving. Risk means laying ourselves on the line. This is personal. We've got to be willing to risk our reputation. We have to be willing to risk our friendships.

Living selflessly for our friends isn't the easiest thing to do. All of us have things that prevent us from being selfless.

What prevents you from being selfless?

_____

_____

_____

There's no pretty way to describe selflessness. Living selflessly is forgetting ourselves on purpose so we can rescue our friends.

We Have to Go All the Way

We have to be willing to walk with our friends all the way. We have to walk with them out of burning buildings and through tough times. We can't just tell them about Christ and then leave them alone. There's a whole chapter devoted to this later, but before we get there, let's just explore the idea.

First, going the extra mile with your unsaved friends means that you're with them at all kinds of times. That means you're present with them when they make some pretty stupid mistakes, and you don't run when they make some sinful choices.

And going the extra mile with your friends means that you walk with them from the point where they have no idea about Jesus to the place where they're completely devoted to Him. That's tough, considering they'll make some silly mistakes and the two of you won't always get along.

We can't stop at just rescuing. We have to go all the way to help our rescued friends begin their walk. It's commitment. It's coendurance—enough endurance for yourself and enough to encourage them to continue. Endurance isn't easy, and having enough for you and your friend seems impossible.

Below, write a few things that keep you from enduring and having a strong walk with God.

_____

_____

_____

_____

_____

_____

Jesus' instructions about friendship seem too hard to follow through on. Giving up our lives for our friends? Really? A lot of times we read that kind of stuff in the Bible and go, "Yeah, whatever. Nice idea; impossible to do." But it's true. We're called to reach into their lives for their sake and at our expense.

We Have to Do It All for the Gospel

Jesus tells us to give up our lives for our friends. One day, a friend almost gave up his life as one of the Twin Towers collapsed. What does any of this have to do with witnessing?

- *If we can't tell our friends about Jesus, then who can we tell?* Our friends are our extended family. They're the people we tell our dreams to. They're the people we cry with, dance with, sing with, and joke with. These people that we're living life with ought to know what is really most important to us.

- *If we can't sacrifice for our friends, who can we sacrifice for?* As you're living life with your friends, and as you're giving things up for their sakes, you realize that the more you surrender, the more your relationship with them is deepened.

Everything I've said so far takes for granted that you actually have friends that don't know Jesus. If you don't, then you've got to ask yourself . . . why not? You are the best person to communicate life-changing truth to people your age. You are God's best chance for reaching your friends who have not responded to

Jesus. You can't leave it up to a youth pastor, senior pastor, or some neato church outreach with big toys or expensive giveaways.

Friendship is the best way to reach people. You already know them. You already have a relationship with them. The question is, are you willing to risk everything so your friends will know Jesus? Can you surrender? If you can't, your friends stand to lose in a big way. If you can surrender—if you are willing to take the risk—your friends could meet the Creator of the universe.

It's all up to you.

chapter eight

Bad Ideas

I live in a medium-sized home that's bordered on two sides by woods. Where we live, it's nearly impossible to get rid of all the brush and overgrowth every year. There's always too many leaves, too many fallen branches, too many old weeds and twigs to give to the garbage collector. Added to that, we don't just own our house, we also own the empty lot next door. All of our property used to be covered with very tall pine trees, which drop all kinds of nasty needles and pinecones all over everything. We affectionately refer to all of the stuff on the lawn (leaves, twigs, and other stuff) as lawn trash.

We'd lived with huge piles of lawn trash for a while when we finally decided that it was time to get rid of all our pine trees. We had about ten huge ones, and the job was going to take all weekend. I called a few guys who came and took the trees away, but they left the limbs and needles for me to clean up. So I called a bunch of my friends over for a limb-burning party. It sounded like a really great idea—we'd just hang out, eat, burn limbs beside my house, and have a great time.

We piled lawn trash all morning, then stopped for lunch. As we were finishing our lunch, two of my friends offered to start burning the pile of trash. (I need to say, in total defense of myself, that I really wasn't paying attention to my pals and where they had placed the burn pile. I was too busy working to pile up more trash and was having a great time with my friends.)

The pile was really big. As my friends lit it, they realized that it was too close to the house. The fire began to rage, and my friends couldn't do anything about it. Soon the fire got so hot and so out of control that it spread quickly to a nearby tree. Fearing the worst, one of us jumped onto the roof of the house and began hosing it down. We were able to save the house, but the tree was really scorched. It's taken years, but it's finally started coming back to life.

We've all experienced a time when we thought we were doing something really great. We make a plan, we go for it, and then it totally flops.

It happens like that often when we're thinking about how we can share Christ with our friends. We set out just to tell them a little about what we believe, and something makes them mad. Then the whole thing goes south from where you planned it. Maybe you set out just to see if your friend was interested in religion, and you ended up setting a huge emotional fire that is still burning.

A Better Understanding of Tolerance

These days, Christians are seen as intolerant and not accepting of others' religious ideas and values. In fact, it's true that we're often unwilling to listen to other religious views. That's because God is jealous. He doesn't allow us to worship other gods, and we pass that jealousy on to others.

But the problem is that the nonbelieving world sees that intolerance and reads it as an unwillingness to listen to an opposing point of view. Nonbelievers refuse to talk to us believers because we so often are inconsiderate of their feelings about God or religion. Our unwillingness to talk is seen as intolerant. The result is that nonbelieving people never engage in a good discussion about the Christian understanding of God because we're seen as intolerant.

God isn't tolerant of other religions. So as believers we want to reflect that standard. But in order for us to get nonbelieving friends to talk, we have to be willing to listen in some way to their beliefs. We can listen to other points of view without agreeing with them and without adopting them.

Our goal? To be present in the lives of our friends. What's that mean? Going places we might never really *want* to go but places that we're willing to go because we want to see our friends get to know Christ. But sometimes there are things we can do that are totally inappropriate—even with the idea that we want our friends to know Christ. As we attempt to take the gospel to places where our friends will hear it, we have to be careful not go places where we could harm ourselves or get into trouble. There *are* wrong places where you could go. How do you know what kind of mistake you *could* make in sharing the gospel with your friends? Keep reading.

Take the following test to see if you understand the importance of being smart about where you try to share Christ.

1. You have a good friend, and she's going to a party this weekend. She's invited you, but you're not sure that you should go. There's probably going to be drinking at the party and possibly some drugs. What should you do?

    A. Go to the party, be there for your friend, and look for opportunities to share Christ.

    B. Stay away from the party and lose an opportunity to tell your friend about Christ.

2. A new guy has moved into your neighborhood. He obviously comes from a very rough family—you know that because you've heard his parents seriously fighting. You think that going over and introducing yourself might be cool. But you're not sure if you'll even be heard or if you'll be safe. What should you do?

    A. Go across the street, risk it, and start a friendship aimed at seeking out what the spiritual condition of the family is.

    B. Stay away, wait for a time when you feel safe or have a good opportunity.

3. A very close friend who attends a cult church has invited you to come to his youth group. This guy never wants to talk

about religion with you, so this is an interesting opportunity. You've been praying for him and think this might be an okay thing to do. What should you do?

A. Go to his youth group.
B. Don't go.

4. One of your unsaved friends uses really rough language. S/he doesn't cuss all the time, but s/he still tosses out a nasty word a few times a day. The more you've been hanging out with her or him, the more you find yourself coming close to slipping up and cussing too. One day, you mess up and use one of your friend's choice words. After you apologize, your friend explains that cuss words aren't in the Bible, so God probably doesn't care what foul words you use. What should you do?

A. Keep on cussing, since the Bible doesn't really say anything about it. And cussing would help your friend relate to you more.
B. Stop using foul language altogether.

5. You've been checking out this guy who you think is really hot. The guy has everything you're looking for: a great smile, fun personality, and his car is kind of cool, too. But he isn't a Christian. The problem is that all the Christian guys you know just aren't what you're looking for in a boyfriend. Even though this guy isn't a believer, you'd really like to go out with him. One of your friends just told you that he's been watching you, too, and she tells you that he's going to ask you out for this weekend. What should you do?

A. Go out with him because he's a hottie.

B. Skip it, because the two of you will probably not agree on some major issues.

The Answers

How'd you do with those questions? The correct answers for some of them are kind of nebulous. Really, all of those questions could be answered differently depending on how comfortable you feel in weird or awkward situations. But here's a short answer to each of them.

Answer 1. Going to a party where there might be alcohol—is it okay? This is one for your parents. In general, if you know that there's going to be something illegal or immoral there, it's probably best to stay away. Doesn't that go against the idea of being present with your friends when they make huge mistakes? Yeah, kind of. But you can't be present for anything illegal as you're sharing the gospel. Too many bad things could happen. An alternate solution might be to go to a party that is said to be harmless, and then be ready to leave when something inappropriate happens.

Answer 2. Going and sharing the gospel with anyone who doesn't know Jesus—even a rough family—is the right thing to do. If there's a family in your neighborhood that doesn't know Jesus then you certainly have the responsibility to tell them about Him. If they're a really rough family and you're not sure about your safety, then find a way to bring them to your house or another safe place.

Answer 3. It's really, really dangerous to go to a church that is considered a cult. While they usually have some elements that appear to be very much like Christianity, the cults in general aren't at all what Jesus meant to build, and they are full of incorrect doctrine and heresy. Should you witness to a friend in a cult? Yeah. But it's probably best to stay away from their youth group meetings.

Answer 4. The Bible is fairly specific about language. Any word that comes out of our mouth that isn't glorifying to God or tears others apart is very wrong. But the question is more than just about language. Is it okay to hang out with people who use really bad language? Ultimately that question is best decided by you and your parents. Here's some advice. With your parents' approval, it's not totally wrong to spend time with people who cuss. The tough thing is that you have to be careful that their words don't drift into your vocabulary.

Answer 5. Is it okay to date non-Christians in the hopes that they'll accept Jesus and become the perfect person? This is often called missionary dating. Here's a clue: The cute guy who isn't a Christian probably won't become a believer just because you're dating. And can you really effectively witness to someone while you're also dating them? Nope. The truth is that dating and witnessing don't go together.

Finding the Balance: Where to Go

It's tough. We want to tell our friends about Jesus, but we don't want to put ourselves at risk or diminish our testimony. How do we manage to do a good job and not mess ourselves up?

Use Caution

Before you go to witness anywhere, stop and think about what you're doing. Jesus went everywhere with the gospel, but He went everywhere because He was all powerful and could handle anything. You're not all powerful. There are things that you can handle and things that will handle you. Always think:

- Will this situation hinder my ability to be truthful with people about who God is and what He can do in their lives?
- Will I be tempted to stumble in my walk if I go hang out with that person?
- Will I be in danger?

Get Parents' Permission

Regardless of what you want to do or where you want to go, you've always got to ask your parents what they think about where you're planning to take the gospel or who you're planning to witness to. Your parents might have been where you are planning to go and might possibly have some great advice to offer you.

Finding the Balance: What to Say

Beyond being careful about where you go with the truth, you've got to be careful about what to say. Here are some examples:

Example 1. You're hanging out with a good friend who's unsaved. He looks at you and begins talking about the party last week. He lays out a long story about how he got drunk and was sick the whole next day. Your response is to tell him how wrong that is and how he'll probably go to hell for living like that. Is that the right thing to say?

Example 2. Your best friend just told you that she's going to begin praying every day. She's decided that it'll help her focus on studies, and she hopes that it'll bring her a sense of peace.

You counter with a "God can't hear your prayers unless you know Jesus. And since you don't know Jesus, prayer isn't going to do you any real good." Is that the right thing to say to your friend?

Both of these situations show the totally wrong thing to say. Why? Because even though it's okay to be honest with people, we've got to learn to tell the truth without damaging people. How do we do that?

The Power of Timing

Often, the right thing spoken at the wrong time can wreck people. We might want to be honest, but if our friends can't handle the honesty right then, our words could ruin any potential for a future conversation. We have to know when to speak, and we have to know what we should say.

How do we get that right? Prayer. Only God knows your friends' hearts, and only He knows when they can handle hearing the whole truth. We've got to ask God for help knowing when to speak, then we've got to ask God to have control over our mouths and minds and use what we're speaking for good in the lives of our friends.

Speaking the Truth in Love

The Bible commands believers to be careful with the truth and to be careful about when we let it loose. Ephesians 4:15 commands believers to speak God's truth in love. Before we let loose a comment about how a friend is living or how wrong their decisions have been, we ought to ask ourselves, "Is what I'm wanting to say a loving statement? Will it come out in a loving way?" If we're sure that we can speak in love, then it's okay. Otherwise, keep it to yourself.

Giving God Our Effort

There's an old story about a small boy who wanted to play the piano. His parents took him to the performance of a major composer. As they waited for the concert to begin, the small boy got more and more impatient. When he couldn't take it anymore and while his parents' weren't looking, the little boy wandered up onto the stage without being noticed by the security guards, sat down at the piano, and began to play "Chopsticks."

The crowd noticed and was amazed. Not amazed at the boy's ability (because he wasn't that great), but at his fearlessness in approaching the great composer's piano. The small boy continued to plunk away at the keys for a few seconds. Then, the world-renowned composer slowly walked across the stage and stood behind him. Totally unaware of his presence, the little boy continued.

As he played, the composer reached his hands around him and began playing a concerto that totally matched his unconventional rendition of "Chopsticks." The more the composer played, the more the little boy's unskilled playing sounded like a masterpiece. When they were both finished, the audience stood and applauded at the composer's ability to make the little boy's song sound incredible.

We mess up. In our attempts to tell our friends about Jesus, we can make some pretty huge mistakes. The good news is that whatever we choose to do and whatever we choose to say, God comes along and creates great music with our effort. What's our role? We've got to be careful. We've got to be loving and cautious. But most of all, we've got to be willing to make mistakes and to let God use our mistakes for His glory. Yeah, we've got to try to not make mistakes, but when we do, God will be there . . . standing right behind us, using our effort in the lives of our friends.

chapter nine

Crafting Your Story

We have three kids who love stories at bedtime. I'm the worst at telling stories. I don't like to read them because I usually begin to zone out about halfway through reading and fall asleep. Usually, my wife reads to the kids and I go in just after the story and give out bedtime hugs. On those rare occasions when I do tuck the kids into bed, and there's enough time for a story, my girls want me to make up a scary story. They'll beg for it, too.

My scary stories probably aren't like most parents' scary stories. I don't have much patience for silly ones where the people in the story stub their toe or just get chased by a man with a golf club. My stories freak my kids out. They still remember the story about "my uncle" who had a zipper in his head, and every night he'd unzip the skin off his face and walk around the house. They remember the story I told about the night my family was out driving and my dad decided to take home a stranded stranger whose house was at the very end of a long, scary dead-end street. You'd think after loads of scary stories my kids would get the hint that they're going to be freaked out. You'd think they'd start crying *before* I start the story. Still, they beg for me to tuck them in. I guess they love my stories.

But that's typical of kids. In fact, everyone loves a good story. Television executives know the power of the story—that's why show after show has at least two or three different stories running parallel throughout each episode. Millions of novels sell each year. People love a good story.

As believers, we can take advantage of the power of the story. If children are drawn to them and TV watchers love them, then we ought to explain what God has done in our lives through an effective story. When we do that well, people are interested and lives can be changed.

Do you want to reach your friends with a great story—the story of your life? The best place to start that is to begin working on your testimony.

What's a Testimony?

A testimony is just like a report. It's a story about what God has done in your life. Like last year, when you went on vacation and had an awesome time skiing in Aspen. You met some really hip movie stars and when you got back you bragged to your friends about all the fun you had while they were bored at home. You told them the testimony (story, report) of your trip because something awesome happened to you, and you wanted to tell someone.

Testimonies are often used to explain the validity of things. They explain how true something is: If it's worked in your life, it must work in someone else's. They also help package essential truth in a way that's easy for people to understand.

What Isn't a Testimony?

A testimony *isn't* a list of all the perfect things you've done, all the awesome experiences you've had with God, and all of the other people you've converted because of your experiences with Jesus. A testimony can have those elements in it, but it's not a chance for you to show off to someone who doesn't know Christ.

A testimony *isn't* full of words people don't understand. Don't try to impress someone with your knowledge of theological vocabulary. Avoid "sanctification," "justification," "washed in the blood," "living in the light," and other Christianese.

A testimony *isn't* an opportunity for you to package all of the truth you've learned growing up in church into a single speech where you tell your story and ram truth into someone's brain.

A testimony *shouldn't* be confusing. Your testimony should make sense to you and your best friend before you ever go out and tell someone else about it.

A testimony *isn't* a fabrication of things you wish you had done before you met Christ. And it's not a bunch of lies about all of the amazing things you've done since meeting Him.

Like we said earlier, a testimony is just the result of an experience that you've had with God. Just like a vacation report to your friends, a testimony gives the basics of the way you were before meeting Christ, how you met Him, and how you've lived since.

Putting Your Testimony Together

Honestly, it can feel kind of overwhelming to put together the story about what God has done in your life. After all, how do you pick out just the right stuff? How do you know what things are important to include? How do you know what to leave out? Even though it can be difficult, it's not impossible. Take the next several minutes and answer the following questions:

1. What were you like before you met Christ?

Most of us have a life we lived before meeting Christ. Whether we met Him at the age of four or fourteen, we had experiences before knowing Jesus. As you begin to think about putting your story together, it's important to paint a picture of what your life was like before Christ. What was your family like? How did your siblings treat you? What things were important to you before you met Jesus? What family difficulties did you experience? If you were saved at a very young age, consider using these lines to create a complete family picture. How did your parents influence your life? Were your grandparents believers? How did that impact you? Use the space below and write everything you feel is important.

_____

_____

_____

_____

_____

_____

_____

_____

_____

_____

2. How did you meet Christ?

The best part of your story comes when you've met Jesus. This is the pivotal moment where your life changed forever. There are three very distinct elements to this moment. *"What happened?"* basically covers the event. Were you at a church service? Were you at a retreat? Were you alone in your room? Whatever the circumstances, it's important to explain the basic situation. *"How did you feel?"* gets at the heart of who you are. Some people experience a huge surge of emotion when they become Christians. Others aren't emotional at all. Both are okay! *"What changed?"* is a chance for you to describe the immediate experience after your conversion. Was there any immediate change? Were you able to completely ignore a sin that held you back for forever?

Think through these three areas. Use the lines provided to completely explain as much as you can.

What happened?

_____

_____

_____

_____

_____

_____

How did you feel?

_____

_____

_____

_____

_____

_____

What changed?

_____

_____

_____

_____

_____

3. What has your life been like since you met Christ?

This part of your story explains the results of your salvation. If Jesus has moved into your life, a change has taken place. You've lived that change since you became a Christian. This is your chance to explain how Jesus has changed you. Use these lines to craft the final part of your story.

What effect has Jesus had on your life?

_____

_____

_____

_____

_____

_____

_____

What struggles do you continue to face? No one is perfect. Take some space and write down some of the things in your life that aren't perfect. Be sure to be as honest as you feel you can.

_____

_____

_____

_____

_____

_____

_____

After You've Put It Together

If you've completed the exercises above, you owe yourself a huge congratulations! Putting together your own salvation story isn't always easy, and putting one together is really only half the work. Once you've crafted it, what do you do?

You've got to practice it. Every good story has a great storyteller. Great storytellers practice their stories. They know how to explain the details. They know how to paint pictures, create drama, and frame their story in persuasive ways. You might not be the world's greatest storyteller, but you can become a master at communicating *your* story. Practice is the best way to get good at it. Ask your youth pastor if you can tell your story to him, and then ask him to evaluate it. Tell it to your friends or parents. Take every opportunity you can to get your story out so you can become a persuasive expert at telling people your story of meeting Christ.

Once you've put it together, and practiced it—it's time to decide who you're going to tell it to. It's time to get your strategy together.

chapter ten

One-Person Strategy

I'm no good at sports. This isn't an exaggeration, and I'm not trying to be falsely humble. I'm really no good. I can't make a lay-up. I have no idea what famous sports guys play for what teams, or for what sport either. I'm totally clueless when it comes to sports. But the other day I gained an incredible appreciation for the strategy that's involved in a good game of football.

I was visiting a few of our high school students on their campus for their last high school game. Since I'm not much into sports, I was kind of bored for the first part. Our team was losing, and the people behind us were yelling annoyingly loud. I was uncomfortable. Halfway through the game, I started to catch on. I began to understand the different players and their purposes for being on the field. I think football makes sense in this way—use the big guys to block and tackle, use the small guys to run the ball around, and dude, don't hit the field unless you've got a solid play book.

Witnessing is the same way. Okay, maybe we don't have to have the biggest dudes on the field or the smartest people calling the plays . . . but we do have to have a solid play book. We've got to have a good strategy if we're ever going to get anything done. You want to tell your friends about Jesus? Good. Then you've got to get a game plan. Think of your approach as being stronger when you've got a good idea of who you'll tell, how you'll prepare, how you might begin your spiel, and how you'll follow up.

Why a Strategy?

God honors all of our efforts, right? And He wants us to *constantly* tell others, right? And (the Bible makes this clear) we've got to always be prepared to give a reason for the hope that we have, right?

Imagine that you've just won a million dollars. Thinking that you'd like to help others, you get some of the million in cash—let's say, about ten thousand dollars (not that much money compared to a million, but still . . .). So you get your 10K, and you start to give it away. What's the smartest way to give it away?

A. Take five of your best friends out for burgers, then pile the rest of the cash on a table and leave it there in the restaurant.

B. Be careful. Make sure that the people you're giving it to are legit. Keep a record of where your money goes.

Which one would you pick? These two different options reflect the different ways we attempt to tell others about Jesus.

It's all about being responsible with what we've got, and giving it away in a meaningful, life-changing way.

The Ultimate Goal: A Changed Life

Ever watch late-night television commercials? You know the kind I'm talking about—the half-hour long ones that are completely annoying and are usually devoted to a product almost no one would really be able to use. Every one of those commercials has people in it telling about how awesome the product is, because in some way the thing has changed their lives. It's either made it easier to cope, easier to live, or easier to get something done. The product has changed their lives.

We're after that same change but in a totally different way. We're after a total change in the people we're telling about Jesus. Not the kind of change that's translated into a "Like, dude. Before Jesus, I couldn't get along with my sister, now . . . well . . . we fight less." Nope. We're after the kind of change that invades our friends in every area of their lives and goes deeper than "Now I can get along with people."

As you're thinking about strategy, think, "How can I present the change that's happened to me in a way that will totally change my friends, too?"

As you think about your play book—your strategy for telling your friends about Jesus—here are five essential steps that will help you put it together.

1. Who (pick someone)

Step one . . . first step in getting your play book together is to pick someone you think you can talk to about Jesus. This is probably the most important step. Why? Well, if you pick the wrong person, someone you don't know well, or someone who just won't listen to anything you say, you'll have failed before you begin.

So it's important to be realistic as you think of the person you'd like to witness to. Here's a list of ideas:

- Choose someone you know well. Maybe a best friend or someone who's close to that.
- Pick someone you kind of know but haven't had a lot of opportunities to talk with. This would be someone who wouldn't laugh at you for saying something about Jesus.
- Don't leap out and pursue someone who's openly anti-Christian your first time out.

Below, write the names of five people you already know you'd like to tell about Jesus.

1. _____

2. _____

3. _____

4. _____

5. _____

2. Are you their friend?

There's an extremely old and worn our phrase that goes, "People don't care how much you know until they know how much you care." Translated, that means you can't just go and unload everything you know about God on someone you've just met or on someone whom you've never spent any time with. They have to trust you first. So it's essential that you don't just reach out; you've got to reach into the lives of your friends. You've got to love them. Why? So they'll hear what you have to say. So they'll see that the gospel you preach has made a difference in your life.

Look over the list of friends that you made. Ask yourself, "Who on the list have I demonstrated unconditional friendship type of love to lately? How can I demonstrate unconditional love to these people this week?" Write some ideas.

_____

_____

_____

_____

_____

3. What do they already know?

After listing the people you want to talk to and after showing you've loved them, you've got to decide what to say. But before you do that, you've got to get a grip on what they already know about God, Jesus, and the Bible. How embarrassing would it be for you to go up to someone you think you know, lay out your entire speech and then hear them say, "Umm, you know. You could probably find out a lot more about what we believe if you go with me to my church."

How do you find out what they already know? You've got to listen to them. You can't just walk up to them and say, "Alrighty dudes, now we're going to talk about God. Why don't you just go ahead and tell me what you know about Him." You *could* talk to them like that, but they'll probably just stare at you or slap you.

Instead, try keeping your ears open to answers to these questions:

- What is their opinion of God?
- Do they seem to understand that God exists?
- Do they appear open to talk about spiritual issues?
- Are they searching for answers to some "big" questions (like the reason they exist or the direction their lives are going)?
- Have they ever had an experience with God?

4. What do you need to say?

After evaluating what your friends know, it's important to get a grip on what exactly you need to say. What kind of conversations might you need to have with them? If you need to know more about this right now, you can jump ahead to the next chapter. That chapter gives you all the info you'll need to get a conversation started with a friend.

5. Before, during, after, after, after . . .

The most important part of any activity is the follow through. What makes a good tennis serve? It's the follow through. What makes a good employee? Someone who follows through— who does what they say they'll do.

The same goes for getting your play book together. We've got to have our follow through together. How do you follow through with a friend, after you've begun a conversation about God? Here are some ideas:

Expect interruptions. Let's say you're walking home with an unsaved friend and a conversation about God gets going. When you get home, you usually watch your favorite TV show. You want to go home and watch that, but your friend is asking some real good questions about God. Expect to be interrupted and be willing to give up your plans to help them in their understanding of God.

Look for opportunity after opportunity. Telling your friend about God once doesn't cut it. A million times is a little much, too. Where's the balance? It's not just knowing what to say, it's knowing when to say it. It's knowing how often to drop ideas about God and Christianity into conversations.

Introduce them to other believers. If you don't know Christ, and you're hanging out with other nonbelievers, it's easy to ignore Christians. But if you take your nonbelieving friend to events or places where your Christian friends are, they'll understand even more what being a believer is all about.

Alrighty . . . there's your strategy. Now that you have one, let's talk about how to get together the right things to say. Move on to the next chapter and discover what you need to know to be prepared.

chapter eleven

What to Say

Having a conversation about your relationship with Jesus means just that—having a conversation. Having a conversation with an unsaved friend means just that—having a conversation.

For forever, witnessing has been seen as a one-sided thing. The church has pushed witnessing as more of a speech. Basically, it was seen as something that went like this:

1. Find an unsaved person.

2. Get your Bible.

3. Ask some important questions like, "If you died tonight are you sure that you'd go to heaven?" Depending on their answers, you'd have all kinds of responses.

4. Highlight their sinfulness. Make sure they know that they are sinners.

5. Ask them if they're willing to accept Jesus. If they are, lead them in the "sinners prayer."

There are a lot of problems with this kind of witnessing. First, the unsaved people involved are basically the recipients of a full-frontal assault. Very often, it's as if they have no choice. This kind of witnessing also reduced the important truth of the gospel down to a short conversation between attacker and attacked. It also lends itself to a number-crunching form of witnessing. When you have a lot of brief conversations about God with nonbelievers, it's easy to attempt to pack in as many of these conversations as possible just to impress your friends.

When you look at how Jesus persuaded people, you see a man pursuing people in order to talk with them about their faith. He never approached them with a bunch of spiritual laws, and he never asked them to pray a sinners prayer.

So, how do you assemble your beliefs in a way that you can easily explain to a friend? Think about it this way. Have you ever thought about the three most important ways that God works in and through us? In general God works through our minds, our hearts, and our hands. When we become a believer, God "attacks" each of these three areas. He moves in our hearts or our emotions. He speaks to our mind and helps us understand deeply spiritual things. As a result of what God has done in us, we have to use our hands. We have to make a decision to begin our walk with God. We have to do something.

As you begin to think about how you'd craft an explanation of your relationship with God in a way that makes sense, think of these three areas—heart, head, hand. Here's how it you can do it.

Your Heart—Your Experience with God

If you're a Christian, you've had an experience with God. Your experience doesn't have to be some kind of drastic change, and it doesn't have to be boring either. If you've been changed by God, you've had an experience.

Begin a conversation with an unsaved friend by asking, "Have you ever had an experience with something you didn't completely understand?" or "Have you ever had an experience with God that you can't explain?" Offer your answers to those questions with explanations of some of your experiences with God.

> { **Scriptures to use:**
> John 1:1–14; John 3:16;
> Romans 5:6–8 }

Remember to ask:

- "What experiences have you had with God?"
- "Can you name a time when you've felt close to Him?"

Your Head—Your Understanding about God

Some of us were convinced and then gave our hearts to God. Others of us were drawn to God through our hearts, and then we gave God our minds. However you were drawn to God, your mind was involved in the process at some point.

After you've explained your experience with God and your friend has shared theirs, tell your friend about what you've learned about God. You might have learned about His personality, or His love for you. You might want to share what you've learned about God after explaining your experience with Him, then ask "What things do you already

> { **Scriptures to use:**
> Genesis 2:4–3:13;
> 1 John 4:7–21 }

know about God?" or "What things about God do you not understand?" Be sure to offer answers to your friend about things that
you have learned or don't understand about God.

Remember to ask:

• "Do you already know some things about God?"
• "What do you know about God's personality?"

Your Hands—Your Responsibility Before God

It doesn't matter how God began to draw you to Him; you eventually had to take action. You eventually prayed to receive Him.
When your relationship began, your walk with Him began and so
did your responsibilities as a believer.

When you realize that God has been reaching out to you
through experience and through your mind, you begin to understand that you have a responsibility. You're responsible to make a
decision to live for Him. You're responsible to actually live for Him.
You're responsible to grow in your knowledge of Him. You might
want to share with your friend the responsibilities that you've taken on as a believer.

Scriptures to use:
Romans 3:22–26;
Romans 6:23;
Galatians 5:1–26

Above all, your conversation with
your friend ought to lead him or her to a
decision about God. You might want to
encourage him or her to make a decision about Him based on
some of your conversation about God.

Remember to ask:

• "What do you feel you'd like to do as a result of our conversation?"
• "What kind of decision do you think you need to make
based on what I've said to you?"

How Do You Use the Heart, Head, Hand Idea?

Easy. Simple.

First, ask your friend about a time when they felt like they were close to God or had an experience with Him. If they've not had an experience, offer one of yours by saying, "Can I tell you about an experience I had with God?" and be sure to use the Scripture passages to help explain your understanding about God.

Second, explain to your friend how you understand God. Build into your understanding that everyone has to make a conscious decision to accept Christ and follow Him. Use the passages listed above to help you describe God's love and His creative power to your friend.

Third, explain to your friend that everyone who believes in God needs to make a concrete decision to accept Him. If you believe that God exists, then you need to decide to learn more about Him and discover more about Him daily. You can use the Scripture passages to help your friend understand that everyone sins, and God is willing to forgive.

If you're looking for a easy-to-follow set of steps that will help you share Christ with your friends, use the list above.

- Draw a heart, head, and hand in the back of your Bible to remind you the steps you can follow to lead your friends to Christ.
- Look up some Scriptures that will help you connect your thinking with God's word.

The Basics

As you use the "Heart. Head. Hand." way of telling your friends about Christ, there is other information you might want to infuse into your conversation. If you need a more specific system, or if you need some more information, these following four concepts might help you.

1. Humanity needs relationship.

Back in the Garden of Eden, God created humans with an innate desire to have a relationship with Him. In fact, that's exactly what they had. Genesis is clear about that. Genesis 1–2 doesn't just point out the creation, it demonstrates how God is intimately involved with His creation. We're not just created in the image of God (Genesis 1:26–28), we're created to have a relationship with God.

And it's not just the fact that we're created to have a relationship with God. This is a relationship that we crave. It's something we can't live without. (Hint: This is why people often create other religions or set other humans up as "godlike.")

2. We're living out a broken relationship.

Hanging out in the Garden of Eden, Adam and Eve took the fateful step and broke their relationship with God. They messed up their one-on-one, intimate relationship with their Creator, the Creator of the universe. Genesis 3:1–24 describes the whole thing and the results of what they did.

Their mistake affects us. Their broken relationship with God is our broken relationship with God. In some ways that's difficult to understand; their sin is passed down to our sin, and we are inherently sinful. (We talked about this a bit in the chapter titled "Reality Check." If you want to know more, go back to that chapter.) Where does the Bible say that we're living out the relationship that Adam and Eve broke? Romans

3:23 says that all of us have sinned. There's no exception—
everyone has sinned.

3. God wants to reestablish the relationship.

The amazing thing about history is that it really is the
process of God working out His plan so He can have an intimate
relationship with humanity. After the Fall, God instituted a sacrificial system. Through the sacrifice of certain animals, God and
mankind could have some kind of relationship, though weak and
distant. Humanity's sins could be forgiven, and they could love
God. Later, God sent His Son so that the God-human relationship could be forever restored. John 3:16 makes that clear.

There are two sides to that relationship. God did His work
and sacrificed His Son for us. Our responsibility is to recognize
our sinfulness and ask forgiveness. It's easy to think that we're
not sinful or that we've never actually committed sins. But 1
John 1:8 makes it clear that if we say that we've never committed any sin, we're liars. First John goes on to explain that if we'll
confess our sins, God will forgive and cleanse us.

4. We need to live out the God-human relationship.

We're created to have a relationship with God. We're being
pursued by God to reestablish the broken relationship. What's
our responsibility after accepting Christ? We have to spend the
rest of our lives in an active relationship with God where we're
pursuing Him as much as He's pursuing us. Our lives have to
reflect the Creator—they have to reflect an active pursuit to
know and be like God.

So let's say that you've been talking to your friends about
God. You've helped them understand who God is. They get that

they're sinners, and they're interested in giving their lives to Jesus. What do you do? How do you handle your friends and yourself if they decide to give their lives to God? The next chapter will help you lead your friends to Christ.

Why Beginnings Are So Important

What's the big deal about beginnings? Who cares about how we start a conversation? Well, beginnings are important because they get people interested in what we have to say. For example, let's say a group of friends are standing in line to get lunch at school. They're all standing there, and you walk up to them. How could you begin the conversation with them? Let's look at the options.

Option One:

You walk up to a pack of friends and say, "Hey freaks. I've had a bad day. Stay away from me . . . leave me alone."

Translation:

Can you use this approach to begin a conversation about your relationship with God? Ummm, no. Easy option to avoid, huh? Maybe not as obvious as you might think. Ever had someone want to talk to you about your relationship with God, and you were not in any mood to talk about it? Maybe you'd had a bad day, or whatever. In any case, when you feel awful, rotten, and in no mood to talk about anything with anyone, this is no time to try to start a conversation about God with someone. And if someone wants to talk with you about God when you're in one of these moods, it's best just to say, "All right, look. I'm not feeling the best right now. Could we talk about this a little later?" and hope they'll be willing to talk later.

Result:

Your friends won't care what kind of a day you've had. It doesn't matter if you've had a bad day. When you act mean, your friends will either stay *way* away from you or give you meanness right back.

Option Two:

Total silence.

Translation:

Well, on top of looking like a total freak (not talking to your friends and all), people don't know how to read you. They have no idea how you're feeling. And you put the burden on them to talk to you. This isn't just weird friendship; it's not polite. We all have times when we just do not feel like talking. This goes beyond the previous "I'm in a bad mood" scenario and reaches into the "I'm totally strange" category. Yeah, it's okay to be quiet now and then. But total, prolonged silence is kind of strange.

Result:

Can you witness without saying anything? Well, yeah. There is that whole idea of witnessing with your life . . . and letting your life preach what you believe. However, you can't really back up how you're living verbally if you choose not to talk. Anyway, the no-talk option really isn't an option. You'll come off freaky. Nothing will get accomplished.

Option Three:

"I *know* the truth. I *live* the truth. I am right . . . *always!*"

Translation:

People who are mean, rude, or slightly impolite turn people off. Ever met a know-it-all? You know this person . . . the kind of guy who always has a better story than you do. Always has a better joke. Always thinks s/he knows more about any subject and has no problem telling you how much.

Result:

You might know all kinds of things about the Bible, but it's not necessary for you to make sure everyone knows how much you know. People who act like this come off with a "Dude, you are going to *hell!*" attitude that turns people off and makes them unwilling to hear what you have to say.

Option Four:

"Hey look, I've just learned this really great thing. I want to tell you about it. No, don't walk away; you've got time right now. After all, you never know when you might die. Really."

Translation:

Pushy people are no fun to be around. Ever walked through an electronics store with your parents and noticed how salesmen hound them to buy something? In the same way, you probably can't stand being around someone who's trying to push a product or an idea onto you.

Result:

Can you share the gospel like this? Always trying to break into conversations or push Jesus off onto people like you're selling a product isn't the best way to begin a conversation with your friends. If you attempt to start conversations with your unsaved friends like this, they'll eventually just stop listening to you.

Option Five:

"Hey, what can I do to help you?"

Translation:

Ever met someone who had a knack of helping others? You

know the kind of person I'm talking about. These are the people who always clean up after you. They always offer to stay late and take up the extra slack. They're kind, peaceful, honest, and hard working. This ethic works itself out in every area of their lives.

Result:

Honest people don't just go far in the world, they make huge differences in the lives of others.

Getting a Good Beginning

These ideas are just the tip of the iceberg. Knowing how to start a conversation is important. Sometimes, starting a conversation about God with friends doesn't have to be formal. After all, if you're hanging out with them and just living life, talking about God might flow naturally. But if it doesn't, it's important to know how to get a conversation going. Take a few moments and write down some ideas for getting a conversation about God started.

1. _____

2. _____

3. _____

4. _____

5. _____

Important Middles

If beginning a conversation is important, then the middle is important, too. You've got to be prepared to begin and continue a conversation about Jesus. Test your ability at keeping a conversation going by using these following situations.

Your friend says:

"So, hey. Look. I know what you're saying about God and all, but I need to know more. Just what is so important about sin? I don't feel very evil, and I'm not sure I've really done that many things wrong. Besides, the thought that you need to tell an invisible God that you're sorry for stuff you're not even sure is wrong is ridiculous. Like I said, I need to know more. This stuff just doesn't make as much sense to me as it does to you."

Your response to friends who say this could take on many forms. It's up to you to continue the conversation, help them understand the truth, and move them toward understanding the idea of salvation. So take a moment and write down what your response might be below.

_____

_____

_____

_____

How did you respond to that situation? Here are some possible ideas, along with their results.

Option One:

"Hey, look. Sometimes you've got to take things on faith. God's Word says that you're sinful, and something needs to be done about it. Period."

Translation:

Ummm, heavy-handed, point-blank witnessing doesn't do

much good. Is this a good middle? Really? Think about it. If you were this person and had these feelings, would you want to hear, "Buck up, dude"?

Result:

Your friend will run away—fast. And s/he will run away without understanding what the heck you're talking about.

Option Two:

"Okay. That's neat. Look, I'm still working this God thing out, and, honestly, your questions are way beyond where I am. I think you ought to find someone else to talk to."

Translation:

Your friend still feels lost and alone. If you've built some credibility, then this kind of response will help him or her feel like God might not really care.

Result:

Your friend will stay lost.

Option Three:

"I understand that you've still got some questions. Actually, I don't have this whole thing figured out either. Let's work on this together and see if we can both try and understand this together."

Translation:

Your friend will understand that faith is a journey and that you don't have to understand everything about God to believe in Him. S/he feel like s/he can trust you.

Result:

Your friend might just possibly get to know Christ and have a healthy understanding of Him, but more possibly because you will take the time to be honest and be real.

Making Sure Your Middle Is Solid

Beginning a conversation about Jesus is important. It's equally important that what you say to your friends is true and leads them to a deeper understanding about Christ. What do you need to know to make sure that you keep a good conversation about God going?

- Remember that a discussion about God is better than a sermon. Your friends need to know that you're willing to talk, not ready with a prepackaged sermon about all of the attributes of God. Be willing and ready to *talk* about God not *preach* about Him.

- Know Scripture passages that talk about sin, salvation, and Christian growth. Be ready to share them from memory— even if you just know the gist of them. Your friends will need to hear God's truth, but be careful not to pull out your Bible at every important moment and begin reading with a "Now the Bible says . . ." Know Scripture, and be willing to share and discuss it.

- Be willing to listen to their ideas. If your friends don't know Christ, their ideas might possibly be skewed or unfounded. They need you to listen to them and their ideas without condemning them on every point.

So, let's say that you've been talking to your friends about God. You've helped them understand who God is. They get that they're sinners, and they're interested in giving their lives to Jesus. What do you do? How do you handle your friends and yourself if they decide to give their lives to God? The next chapter will help you lead your friend to Christ.

chapter twelve

What If Someone Says Yes

The scariest thing that ever happened to me started really innocently.

One fall day, when I was about thirteen, my dad took my family to visit some of his friends. One of the people we were visiting had a small motorcycle sitting in his garage. My dad had practically raised me on his motorcycle. I had spent many Saturdays on the back of the seat breathing the fresh air of the Ohio countryside. Standing in the garage that day, looking at the small motorcycle, I remembered my trips with Dad and *knew* I could handle it. I begged and begged and finally was given permission to ride it. I'd never actually been in control of one; the owners knew that but didn't seem to mind.

I sat down on that baby like a pro. I looked good. I was in charge. In my mind, I started the thing, put it in gear, and began to ride around. In reality, I was freaking out. Did I mention that I had never actually driven a motorcycle? Well, my lack of experience and physical inability all went into action the second my dad kick started the motorcycle for me (because after trying a few times, I couldn't start it).

The engine revved every time I twisted the handlebar grip. (I figured out that this was what I needed to do after looking at the hand signals everyone was making.) I felt the power, and I felt powerful. I let go of the clutch, and the thing took off.

The next few seconds were a nightmare. I got scared and twisted my hand, which made the motorcycle go faster. I was freaking out so much that I completely lost control. The bike took control, and I went wherever it wanted to go. It raced toward the neighbor's house, toward their garage, and smacked me into the garage door. I flipped upside down . . . the bike flipped, too. I hobbled away with a seriously cut foot. I limped for days.

There are some things in life that freak us out, or they should. Some things are so scary we hope they never happen. I'll never get on another motorcycle. The thought of it makes me a little queasy.

Witnessing to our friends can make us feel anxious. Some of us are unsure of our ability to answer questions. Others aren't sure about how to approach our friends with our life stories.

But a lot of us freak out when we think about our friends actually saying yes to us. What should we do if they say they'd like to accept Jesus into their lives? What should we say?

The Most Important Things

If you've shared your story with a friend and s/he is ready to accept Jesus, then the next steps are really pretty easy. There are a lot of different ways to approach this important decision with your friend.

One way you might want to approach it is to invite your parent or youth pastor into the situation. If you do this, offer to let your friend talk with the adult, and explain to your parent or youth pastor what's going on and what your friend wants to do.

You might also want to consider asking a few questions just to make sure your friend understands what s/he is doing. Some questions to ask include:

- *Do you understand God's love for you?*

Using chapters 1, 3, and 4, explain to your friend that God loves him or her with an unconditional love. You might want to read Romans 5:6–8 so s/he will understand God's love. Also, take this chance to explain how God intended for them to have a relationship but that sin interrupts that relationship.

- *Are you aware of your sin?*

To help your friend with this question, you can turn to chapters 1 and 4 where it's explained what sin is and what sin does to our relationship with God. You might want to point out that sin is the thing that totally wrecks our relationship with God.

- *Do you recognize your need to have forgiveness for your sins?*

Again, chapters 1 and 4 will help explain why getting forgiveness is important. A really great passage in Scripture to read to your friend is 1 John 1:8. Read that and then explain that since sin is the barrier between us and God, confessing our sin removes the barrier. Then read 1 John 1:9 to show what the Bible says about confessed sin. You also might want to explain to your friend that the only way to heaven is through the forgiveness of sins. The only way to receive forgiveness for sins is to accept Jesus and the forgiveness that He offers. John 14:6 is an awesome passage to read.

How to Pray

After you cover these basic concepts with your friends, it's time to pray. And look, there's no magic here. It's not like if you pray one way they'll be saved but another way they'll miss out. It's vital to remember that what's happening between your friends and God is spiritual. God knows what's happening and isn't concerned that you lead someone in the "correct prayer." What He's watching for is your friend's willingness, his or her forgiven sins, and his or her desire to grow in Him.

What exactly should you pray? You might want to lead him or her in saying something like this:

> *Dear Jesus, I'm sorry for the sins that I've committed. Please forgive my sins and wash me clean. Beginning today, I want to have a new life in You. I want to know more about You, and I want to grow to be more like You. Please help me to follow You every day and in every area of my life. Thank You for forgiving my sins and for making me a new creation. I pray this in Jesus' name. Amen.*

After the Prayer

The next steps are vital. Here's a short list of what you need to help your friend do in the next few days.

*1. You need to help them get a Bible.**

Encourage them to begin reading God's Word, and direct them to one of the four Gospels. As you encourage them to read, offer to read the same stuff they'll be reading. Then, as you see each other at school (or wherever) you will be able to talk with them about what the two of you are reading.

2. You need to encourage them to tell their parents.

Not all parents are willing to hear that their kid has taken this step, so be careful not to push them. But, if their parents are willing to listen and understand their kid's salvation, it's important for them to share it with their parents.

3. You need to help your friend get connected with a church.

You might want to encourage them to go with you to your church. Wherever they choose, you might want to initially encourage them to talk to your youth pastor so your friend can tell someone safe what they've just done.

Most of all, you need to congratulate your friends. They've taken an amazing step, and their eternity has changed. You need to celebrate together. Buy them a soda and hang out for a while . . . you deserve it!

*You can purchase an Extreme Teen Bible *for only $14.99 when you call 1-800-933-9673, x.1 and use the source code:* W101–0849944163

chapter thirteen

Failing and Freaking Out

Christina was about fourteen years old. She had just become a believer, and it was about the same time of the year that her youth group went to Mexico for their annual mission trip. Since she had just become a Christian, she decided to go with the group.

Once they got to Mexico, the deal was pretty simple. Students were supposed to go out with handfuls of tracts and tell people about Jesus. Simple, huh? Except for Christina. She met the world's most difficult witnessee in Mexico.

Christina and the entire group were let loose on an outdoor market with their tracts. They began their job just like their peers did in other parts of the city.

She noticed a guy sitting against a building, looking at the ground. She decided to go up to him and offer him a tract. So she walked over, dropped the tract in his lap, and began explaining it to him. She followed the tract, and hoped that the man was paying attention.

No dice. The man didn't even look up.

Christina got frustrated, but she was determined. So she began again. Basically, she retold him all the stuff she'd said the first time. She raised her voice, got more emphatic. She really got into her speech.

He didn't even flinch.

So Christina tried a new tactic. She read the tract very loudly. In fact, she was yelling it. When the guy didn't respond, she went beyond frustrated and got really angry. Christina threw the Spanish tract in the lap of the unresponsive man, kicked him, and ran off.

Christina's leader was watching. As Christina ran off, her leader walked up to her and asked her what happened. Through tears of frustration, she told him the whole thing. He listened intently.

When she was finished, her leader broke the news to her. "Christina," he began, "that guy is blind and deaf. He couldn't respond to you because he couldn't see or hear you."

Christina felt really stupid. So without thinking, she ran over to the man, picked up the tract, and apologized.

It doesn't matter how much you prepare or how many times you practice. As you begin to share your faith with your friends, you're going to make mistakes, and you might just freak out. Don't think that you won't—because you will. And it's best to prepare for those mistakes now.

Freaking out might happen. You might fail, too. So let's talk about what happens if you freak out or if you fail. We'll hit them one at a time.

What Does It Mean to Fail?

Look, before you talk about failure, you've got to talk about what the word *failure* means. Why? Because sometimes failure can be good.

You want to know something weird? When you look into the Bible and search for the meaning for the word *failure,* it's kind of difficult. That's because the Greek and Hebrew people didn't have a one single word that meant "to fail." They associated failure with concepts like "to be at an end" or "to become ineffective."

In our day, we do understand the word *failure.* But our idea of failure has been conditioned by some really awesome men in history. Great people in history have experienced failure. Who?

Guys like Abraham Lincoln. Lincoln was born into poverty and was uneducated. He tried to marry, but the woman he proposed to turned him down. He lost elections twice before eventually getting elected to the House of Representatives. Later he ran for the Senate but lost. He ran for the office of vice president but didn't get elected. Lincoln knew failure, and it never deterred him.

Thomas Edison lived with the same healthy view of failure. It's said that Edison tried over ten thousand experiments before he eventually succeeded in the invention of the light bulb.

Check these guys out! How do you define failure based on their lives? Well, if loads of their experiments didn't work and they weren't thought of as failures, then we're not failures if we attempt something and it doesn't work out. If we attempt to tell our friends about Christ and they don't respond, that's not a failure.

A Better Way to Look at Failure?

Is there a better way to view failing? Can we even use the word *failure* when we're talking about sharing the gospel? We can talk about failure in the sense that there are things that go wrong when we're trying to tell others about God. Even though we honestly try, sometimes things do go wrong. And even though failure is a harsh word and it might not necessarily describe all of the mistakes that happen, let's talk about some of the things that can go wrong and why things often do go wrong.

Mistakes happen because we are human.

Check out your hand for a moment. Do you see it? It's made of flesh and blood. You're a human being. You're not perfect. Don't even try to think that you're impervious to making mistakes.

Because you're human, you need to realize that despite making mistakes, you're not responsible for your friends' decisions. Some friends will choose Jesus; some won't. Whatever they decide, it's not something that's under your control.

So if they don't decide to follow Christ, it's not your fault. If they do, it's not to your credit. And most of all, if you mess up telling them about Jesus, you're a human being. You're limited. You'll makes mistakes. God still loves you regardless of your mistakes.

We fail because the person we're trying to talk to isn't interested.

Remember before when we were talking about how your friends' decisions aren't up to you? That same logic applies to this one, too.

You can live boldly for Jesus all you want. You can tell the truth all you want. You can have all the right Scriptures ready to nail them with the truth. But if your friends aren't ready, then they're not ready. And if you attempt to tell them about Christ and they *aren't* ready, they'll not respond in the way you expect, and you'll feel like a huge failure.

You can avoid these feelings by accepting that their decisions aren't up to you and being prepared that they might not be as ready as you think.

We make a big mistake when we use confusing language or aren't prepared.

Christians are notorious for speaking in ways that nonbelievers don't understand. It's easy to do that. We think that everyone thinks about God the same way we do, especially when we've grown up in the church. And we think that everyone, nonbelievers included, describe God and eternity the same way we do. In fact, we're often confused that our nonbelieving friends don't understand what we're saying.

We fail because we don't try.

The worst kind of failure is not trying. Remember the famous Americans we talked about in the beginning of this chapter? Remember Christina, the girl who kicked the deaf guy? Were they failures?

They weren't. They may have made mistakes, but they weren't failures. They experienced setbacks, but they didn't fail. Had they not tried, that would have been failure. And notice that through their setbacks and mistakes, good things happened—especially with the famous Americans—because they looked at their setbacks and kept moving.

If we don't try, we've failed. If we don't take some kind of step to tell our friends about Jesus, we've failed in a huge way. What's the worst kind of failure? Not caring enough about our friends to step out, try something a little tough, and tell them about Jesus.

And Now . . . Freaking Out

Christina freaked and kicked the deaf guy. By doing that, she reacted and harmed the guy. She tried and tried and tried—but in the end, the guy didn't respond. That freaked her out.

We get freaked out too. Maybe not because we wind up trying to convert a deaf guy, but possibly because we are trying and the other person isn't cooperating.

Freaking out when you're telling someone about Jesus looks like a variety of things. Some of them might include being:

Speechless. We get so confused, we can't say anything. We can't think clearly, and we feel totally (mentally) helpless.

Angry. Like Jenny, something is happening that is out of our control, and we get angry. This anger comes out in crying, laughter, yelling, and other things.

Out-Matched. Sometimes getting freaked out, combined with speechlessness, means that the other person's argument or discussion wins out. We can't think . . . they keep talking . . . our arguments don't make sense, and they "win."

Sprint. Fear and freaked-outness can take over, and the desire to flee becomes super huge. We get so afraid that all we want to do is run away.

When we freak out, our attempts become useless, and our emotions take over. When that happens, all of our work, all of our attempts, and all of our planning becomes useless. How can we prevent ourselves from freaking out, losing it, and wasting our efforts?

Planning. If you knew someone was going to question you about your faith and you couldn't avoid it, wouldn't you prepare for it? Wouldn't you get really ready for someone you knew who was going to possibly give you a hard time about your testimony? You'd be silly *not* to prepare a little more.

So take a few minutes to do some logical thinking. Let's say, you're going to tell someone about your relationship with Jesus in the hopes that they'll at least *begin* to think a little more about *their* relationship with God.

What Are the Possible Responses?

Knowing how someone might respond helps you stay calm. Below (and with your testimony in mind) think through five of the possible responses someone might give to your testimony.

1. _____

2. _____

3. _____

4. _____

5. _____

Now, think through your possible responses to each of these. For example, if you wrote, "Might totally make fun of me in front of our friends, and I'd feel stupid" as one of their possible responses, then you might write as one of your responses, "I'd smile and laugh it off with them." Each of your numbered responses ought to match the responses you wrote above. For example, your #3 ought to be a response to the idea you wrote on #3 above.

1. _____

2. _____

3. _____

4. _____

5. _____

Does that help? It should. You might not feel like it now, but a time will come when someone will react poorly to what you have to say, and you don't want to be caught off guard. What do you do with the ideas you just wrote out? Write these responses on another sheet of paper and put it in your purse, wallet, or Bible. Keep it with you so that if something happens, you'll be better prepared.

Getting freaked out is no fun, and no one wants to feel like a failure. While you can't prevent every bad thing that happens, you can be prepared. God doesn't want you to go out without being successful in some way. And He can't stand it when you don't feel successful when you tell your friends about Jesus.

chapter fourteen

Long-Haul Evangelism

I know a lady who prayed me into knowing Jesus before she had ever met me. I know a couple who prayed that I'd know Christ twenty years before they met me. Let me tell you about it.

First, the lady.

When I was young, I was a wreck. My parents were divorced, and I was angry about it. I would go jogging each night to get my energy and my anger out—so I wouldn't unleash it on my mom or my sister. Growing up in a divorced family is tough.

One summer, a young guy came to a local church to serve as the summer youth intern. He didn't invite me to attend church; he invited me to help him do his laundry and go running with him. Slowly, through loads of laundry and miles of running, this guy and I formed a relationship. For me, it was just a friendship with a guy. For him, it was a prayer request for his mom.

This guy's mom was an amazing prayer warrior. He described her as someone who "bugged God about it until she got an answer." So when this summer youth intern and I began to hang out, he told his mom and she began to pray for me. She prayed all summer for my salvation. Eventually, she got exactly what she was bugging God about.

Now, the couple. My wife has amazing parents. They've got to be the most spiritually minded people I've ever met. They have a deep understanding of the impact that prayer makes on people, and they're not afraid to use that impact on others.

Before I was born, they prayed for their daughter's husband. They prayed for his protection and that he'd be a man that knew Jesus. They prayed all through my wife's growing up years, but they prayed especially hard (and prayed a lot) during my wife's teen years. Each morning they would come together as a couple and lift up each of their daughters. When they got to Jacqui, they'd pray for her future husband. They didn't know it, but at the time they were praying for me.

Here's the weird thing.

One day (years after we were married) I was talking with my wife's parents about the times they'd been praying for Jacqui's future husband. They were able to recall specific times and seasons where they'd been certain to pray. They remarked that they prayed during specific years of my wife's early adulthood. Those same years that they were praying especially intently were the same years I was going through specific difficulty, and the same year when I accepted Christ. Hundreds of miles away from them and at the same time, my youth pastor's mom was "bugging" God for my salvation. I didn't have a chance.

That's long-haul evangelism. No, it's not specific to praying for a future spouse, and it's not something to just give to your mom and have her do. Long-haul evangelism is about keeping up your witnessing and your evangelism strategy for more than a week. It's about continuing in your efforts to win your friends long after the emotional rush to get them to heaven dies down. Notice what my youth pastor's mom did? She bugged God for my salvation. Remember what my wife's parents were doing? They were persistent over many, many years.

How do those examples of persistence translate into long-haul evangelism for you and me? I think the best example of persistence is the life of Paul. Remember that guy? Here's a little review.

Paul was a great Jew. He'd achieved everything a great Jew should have. He'd been schooled by the best. He'd risen through the ranks of Jewish society to become one of the leading men of his time. When Jesus' followers had become too bold and had grown too large and way too effective, Paul's persistence went into action—he mercilessly pursued Christians and persecuted them.

And then he met Jesus. Paul pursued Jesus with the same persistence that he had captured and killed believers. Once he met Christ, he went away and studied about Him. Then with his knowledge of Jesus and the experience he'd had, Paul set out to tell the world. His persistence mechanism went into action, and he pursued nonbelievers with a relentless passion. He went on at least three very long, very tiring missionary journeys. In those journeys he traveled hundreds of miles both by land and by sea—each mile because he was passionate about sharing the gospel. If the journeys weren't tough enough, Paul was frequently jailed for his outspoken persistence. While in prison, Paul wrote letters to people he'd visited to help further their understanding of Jesus. He took people he was discipling with him on his journeys.

The Short Haul

Paul was the king of long-haul evangelism. He was the poster child for endurance. It can be different for us. Not all of us have the same ability to be passionate 100 percent of the time. We get tired. We get discouraged. And we buy into the idea that because we're finite and human, the short-term solution to telling our friends about Christ is the best option. We believe that it's okay to give them four laws they have to know and respond to, lay out our facts, and then move on. This is easy for us, since it requires little effort and makes it their decision, not our problem. If after a few minutes they don't agree or give in, we've done our best and their eternity is their problem.

But Paul's life and endurance demonstrates that evangelism is best lived over the long term. If this is true, then why do we opt for the easy-out, short-term evangelism strategy?

1. We choose the easy route because it takes *less time*. Face it, traveling with your friends from eternally lost to accepting Christ can take a long time. If we don't feel we have the time, it's just easier to lay out "truth" and let them decide.

2. We choose the easy route because it takes *less effort*. If we just have a list of things we want to convince our friends of, then we don't have to examine other truths or be prepared to handle other ideas. What we believe isn't challenged, and we feel safe.

Short-haul witnessing is easy and doesn't challenge us at all. It's also contrary to how Paul lived and how Jesus demonstrated helping others understand truth. But how do we get the whole long-term evangelism thing together? How do we actually live a long-haul witnessing strategy? There are no easy answers, but here are some ideas that will help you live the gospel before your friends over the long term.

Your friends are your mission. You have to walk with them through life.

We've hinted at this, so let's just come out and say it: The most essential element of a long-haul evangelism mentality is knowing your target. Knowing your target helps you craft your message, and it helps you prepare in advance for possible objections your friends might have. But knowing who you're going to tell your story to also gives you a goal. You are the best messenger for your friends. They'll listen to you more than they'll listen to anyone. Since they'll most likely listen to you, they're the people you need to reach. They are your mission. And because they are your mission, it's up to you to walk with them through life. Walking how far through life? For forever. Sometimes you have to plant a seed, drop a truth, and then move on. It might take years for that seed to sprout. It might be your mentioning your relationship with God to them during your junior year, then following up on that through your senior year, and continuing to keep in contact with them through college or beyond. Regardless of how long it takes, you've got to walk with them, offer truth along the way, and pray for them constantly.

You will get tired because you are a human being. Stay close to other believers.

You are not made of steel. You are not an autonomous being who is not affected by other people's reactions, someone else's bad mood, lack of sleep, or fear. You are human. And because you're finite, you'll get tired along the way. Telling others about what you believe is mentally tiring! Expect to hit some rough spots.

How do you avoid the temptation to give up when you're tired? One of the best ways is to surround yourself with friends who know Christ and are sharing Jesus with their friends too. If you're working together to reach out to your unsaved friends, then you'll be able to support each other when you're tired. Also, going to worship every week helps. Worship refreshes our souls, and that helps when we're at the end of our energy and we're digging from the bottom of the barrel.

You will experience prison. You'll need to know God as completely as possible.

Not only will you get tired, but you'll also experience some fairly rough stuff along the way. People will yell at you. People will disagree with you. Friends will choose not to follow Christ. Those things—every negative witnessing experience—can feel like a little prison. It can make us feel claustrophobic. These little jail cells are built by Satan, and God hates it. When people get upset with our message, Satan uses their anger against us. Through that, he causes us to spiral into insecurity, and he uses that insecurity to prevent us from ever witnessing to anyone again. It's tough to believe God over Satan, and sometimes Satan's discouraging comments are so much louder than God's encouragement that even if we want to believe what God is saying, we can't hear Him.

That's why it's essential to always stick close to God. We've got to know Him so completely that we know His voice. How do we do that? We've got to devote ourselves to studying His Word and to praying. If we know God's Word, then we know His plans and we know His truth. If we spend time in prayer, then we've made an other-worldly connection with our Creator. Giving God time every day both to study His Word and to pray are important tools in long-haul witnessing strategy.

Interested in a long-haul witnessing strategy? Willing to work with your unsaved friends over a long period of time? Then you've got to be devoted. It's a long journey, but it's an important one. Staying committed to God first and then to your friends' salvation will help ensure that your devotion to your friends' salvation might possibly end in success.

chapter fifteen

Being Bold

There's an old story about a guy who became a Christian at a homeless shelter. The man was a drunk and lived the usual life of a drunk homeless person: Always dirty. Always begging for money. Always wasted.

After he became a Christian, the man was equally well-known but for entirely different reasons. Joe left his selfish ways behind and became one of the most caring people associated with the shelter. Joe was always hanging out at the shelter and was always willing to do what needed to be done. Nothing was beneath Joe. He was willing to clean up puke left behind by a sick alcoholic. He'd happily scrub toilets. Whatever the task, Joe could be counted on by the homeless men of the mission to do it. His love and service were well-known and made a difference in the lives of the men of the shelter.

One evening, when the director of the mission was delivering his evening sermon, one man decided that God was calling. He slowly walked forward, fell at the altar, and cried out to God for help to change. He kept crying, "Oh God, make me like Joe! Make me like Joe! Make me like Joe!"

Before long, the director said to the man, "Sir, I think a better prayer would be, 'Make me like Jesus.'"

The drunk replied with a confused look on his face, "Is he like Joe?"*

You know, we get so confused about having the right words . . . and that *is* important. And we get so confused about what to say—when, how, where. We get concerned that our friends are ready and that we will mess things up. When the reality is that our friends (and the world for that matter) are dying (literally) to see the gospel. It's not enough to have all the right words and phrases together. We've got to be living it. Joe served out of gratitude for the change that had taken place in his life, but the result that his life was loudly proclaiming was the change and the effects of the gospel on the life of a believer. The result of Joe's life was that others wanted to be changed.

Right now, take a look at your life, an honest look at how you live. Does your life scream the change that's taken place?

Let's evaluate.

1. Why Living It Is Important

It's easy to debate the importance of words over actions. After all, if all we do is live boldly and never say anything, people

*Rice, Wayne. *More Hot Illustrations for Youth Talks*. Grand Rapids: Zondervan, 114–115.

might not learn basic truths about Christianity. And if all we do is talk about Christ and don't demonstrate it with our lives, we end up with a good speech but no follow up.

Living boldly for Christ is important because it allows others to see that what we proclaim to be true is actually true, and it's able to be lived. It's important that those around us who don't know Christ *hear* what we have to say. And because of that, we need to perfect what we say and make sure that it's clear. But it's also important that those around us *see* what we're saying, too.

Most Christians fall into one of two main camps: They either talk loudly or they live loudly. Few of us get both right all of the time. Here's a profile of each kind of person.

Loud Talkers. These people are willing to tell you everything they know about God, the Bible, and spiritual issues. They've got an answer for everything. They seem to be quick thinkers. They appear to be people who have done loads of research on every possible topic in the Bible. These people believe that all of their convincing knowledge will convert people for God's kingdom. The problem is that facts, laws, and impersonal truths—while they're neat—don't help people understand how all of the truths are supposed to be lived out. Facts by themselves are useless.

Bold Livers. These people know how to live rightly, and they do it very well. They've got all of the biblical laws memorized, and they make sure they live them to perfection. These people think that others are watching them 24/7 and that their lives will convert people by the thousands. The problem with this is that just living it isn't enough. Our friends can't pick up on a message . . . they've got to hear us talking about why we live different.

Doing Both. Is it possible to do both? Can we live loudly and talk loudly? We can. Combining these two is the most essential and effective way to evangelize our friends. How do we get both working together? We start by looking at how we live. Since we've spent a lot of time already in this book getting what we say together, let's work on getting our lives to boldly proclaim Jesus. If we're going to do that, we've got to begin evaluating ourselves.

2. Taking a Hard Look at You

Evaluating your actions isn't the easiest thing to do. We all want to look at ourselves like we're the most perfect believer that ever walked the earth. The truth is that most of us are not nearly as awesome as we think we are, and often our actions don't match the message we preach. If we're going to get our actions in sync with our words, we've got to evaluate what we've done in the lives of others.

Since evaluating ourselves isn't easy, I'd like you to do the following two steps.

First, from your perspective take a look at the things you think you're doing. Answer the following from your perspective:

• One person you've selflessly loved this week: _____
• One person you've selflessly served this week: _____
• One person you've prayed for this week: _____

Second, from another person's perspective write a description of how you live. Imagine that you're someone else, studying your life. What kinds of things might you see about you? Write down a few short sentences about what others might say about your life below.

_____

_____

_____

_____

_____

_____

_____

_____

Did you have a hard time answering those questions? Was it tough trying to write about your life from another person's perspective? What did you learn from looking a little closer at your actions? What aspects of your life might you want to try to improve on? Think for a moment, then write down as many as five things that you'd like to change about your outer witness.

1. _____

2. _____

3. _____

4. _____

5. _____

If it's true that our actions speak louder than our words, then we've got to do everything we can to improve our outward walk with Christ. Not to impress God, but to make an impression on others for God's glory. The apostle Paul makes this point abundantly clear when he wrote a letter to the church at Corinth. Paul says,

Dear brothers and sisters, when I came to you, I did not come preaching God's secret with fancy words or a show of human wisdom. I decided that while I was with you I would forget about everything except Jesus Christ and his death on the cross. So when I came to you, I was weak and fearful and trembling. My teaching and preaching were not with words of human wisdom that persuade people but with proof of the power that the Spirit gives. This was so that your faith would be in God's power and not in human wisdom. (1 Corinthians 2:1–5)

Paul's message was passionate and transformational, but even Paul didn't rely on the words he spoke as much as on the actions he lived. Notice the things that Paul admits that he doesn't use or rely on: fancy words or superior wisdom. Paul doesn't seem to rest on knowledge. Apparently, he relied on something greater—Jesus and His crucifixion. You can't help but think that Paul would have been the ultimate server. Remember who he was before meeting Jesus? He tortured and killed Christians. Paul's conversion was certainly dramatic, but it was also something that he never got over. His transformation impressed even himself, and he never forgot the moment that he met Christ. It was a central theme in his sermons; it was central in his letters, too. That change led Paul to do some amazing things. He served and gave of himself because he had been rescued. And he never forgot his Rescuer.

- Eloquent words are nice but don't accomplish much.
- Being the know-it-all is cool for our self-esteem but doesn't help our friends really grasp who Jesus is.
- Serving in love is the best way to let our lives shout the change that has taken place.

So think about it. Is serving others tough for you? Is living out your faith difficult? Write out the things that prevent you from living your faith boldly before your friends.

_____

_____

_____

_____

_____

_____

_____

_____

Read back over your list. Are there silly things there like fear or uncertainty? Are there things on the list that your parents or youth pastor could help you work through? What things on the list could be solved through prayer and by turning them over to God?

It's important to look over the things that prevent you from living a faith that's out in the open. So take a moment, look over the list you just made, and think through the other things you've read in this chapter. What in your life needs to change in order to live out your faith in front of your friends. Write some of your ideas below.

_____

_____

_____

_____

_____

_____

_____

_____

Sometimes the Best Message Is Willingness

It's important to live your belief in Christ boldly. Not all of us can do that right now. For some of us, it takes a while to get our lives together. We have a long list of public sins we need to shed, or we're hanging with a group of people who make it impossible for us to live our faith boldly. What do we do in the meantime while we're getting our lives together?

We live our willingness. Willingness is simply responding to the situations that God lays before us in the hopes that we'll lead someone to Christ. Being willing to offer Christ to someone is often our most effective evangelism strategy.

I know a guy who has the idea of willingness down to a science.

Jonathan was traveling with a singing group who traveled all over the world. As his group was on their way to one of their overseas locations, they had several hours off in an airport in a foreign country. With the time off, Jonathan decided to relax and walk around.

As he was looking around, Jonathan ran into a man who lived in the airport. The guy's story went something like this: Several years ago, he had been traveling through the airport on his way from one country to go to live in another country. For whatever reason, he'd become stranded in the airport. Because he was a foreigner and didn't have a visa, he wasn't allowed to leave the airport. He was out of money and couldn't afford to purchase another ticket to leave the country. He was stuck in the airport while the government decided what to do with him. The more they talked, the more the subject turned to religion. The man was a bold Muslim witness and told Jonathan exactly what he thought. Jonathan wasn't shy about what he believed either, but instead of debating beliefs with the guy, he gave the man the small New Testament he'd picked up earlier that day. He gave it to the man with the encouragement just to take a look at it. The man promised that he would.

Several weeks later, the group was back in the same airport, and Jonathan decided that he'd go and look for the man who had his Bible. It didn't take long for Jonathan to locate him. He was still living in the airport. Still in government limbo. Still waiting for the opportunity to move on with his life.

The man recognized Jonathan as he approached, and, upon seeing him, he walked quickly toward him, talking the whole way.

As the two got reacquainted, the man confessed that he didn't have his Bible. Actually, he'd begun reading it and had worked his way well through it, but a few days earlier he'd met a fellow Muslim and stuck up a conversation with him. As they talked, their conversation turned to the Christian religion and the Bible Jonathan had given him. The man asked if he could borrow the Bible to read more about the Christian religion and Jesus. The airport man loaned the Bible to the guy who promised to return it on his way back through the airport a few days later.

Did Jonathan ever get the Bible back? Nope. Did he ever see the guy stranded in the airport again? Nope. In fact, Jonathan never really got closure to the Bible incident. We'd love a "and both dudes became Christians, and everyone lived happier" kind of ending. It'd make this a really cool story, wouldn't it? But even if we don't know what happened to these guys, Jonathan's willingness to offer truth at any time (even in an airport very far from home) demonstrates how important it is to be willing to tell anyone, at any time.

Words? Yeah words are important.

A message? Yeah, a well-thought-out message is important, too.

But more than anything, you've got to be willing. You have to be prepared to tell people about Christ by the way you live, by your willingness.

The power of the changed life. It's important. It's powerful. What's more powerful? The power of a changed life that serves everyone it meets. The power of a believer who constantly and regularly puts others ahead of herself so that through her actions the gospel is preached in a way words could never touch.

That's bold living.

chapter sixteen

Get It On

Is it all worth it? Really?

That's a good question. Think of all the things that I'm asking you to put on the line.

Your friendships. Throughout this book I've made it sound easy to tell your friends about Jesus. Your friends might just be the most difficult person to tell.

Your status. Tell one person at your school about what you believe, and you'll be instantly labeled. People will watch every move you make. They'll listen to every word that falls out of your mouth. Chances are, some of them won't be standing around to tell you how much they like your story.

Your spiritual life. As you explain your beliefs, you're going to give and give of yourself. You'll get tired. You'll be concerned about your friends. It'll take extra time and effort to keep yourself spiritually fueled.

Is it worth putting your status at risk? Is it worth risking a friendship? That's a hugely personal question, isn't it? I mean, regardless of the *fact* that your friends need to hear about Jesus, it's still a very personal choice to take the step to tell your friends about Christ.

Yeah, it's worth it. How do you know?

One summer our youth group went to Mexico on a mission trip. Before we went, we did all of the typical pre-mission-trip prep stuff. We learned how to build things, we learned how to tell little children about Jesus, and many of us had to go through Spanish classes. There was one guy, Paul, whose parents are from Peru, and they spoke Spanish around their house. Paul was used to hearing Spanish all the time. But, even with the Spanish he heard at home, Paul claimed that he couldn't speak any Spanish.

Every class was difficult for those of us who didn't get Spanish, and even more difficult for Paul. It seemed that he didn't remember much Spanish and got more and more annoyed about having to go to Spanish classes.

When we finally got to Mexico, Paul wasn't much help. We'd meet nationals, and Paul would act like he couldn't understand them. Each day, as we built or wandered the streets of Matamoros attempting to tell people about Jesus, Paul acted like a lame duck. Now and then he'd help, but mostly he was quiet while our translator did all the work.

One day we were all freaking out. It was the big day when each group had to split up and go house to house and witness. We had to break into two groups, but we only had one translator. So while one group went into a home and witnessed, the other group walked around and prayed for them.

I started with the praying group, and the witnessing group

was taking forever. As they walked, looking for someone to talk to, we walked and prayed for what felt like forever. Pretty soon we got lost, and the other half of our team was nowhere in sight. We paused for a moment and attempted to get our bearings. As we talked and tried to decide, I saw that Paul was missing. After looking around, I noticed him standing next to a fence, talking to a young lady on the other side.

We all walked over to Paul, totally expecting them to be talking in English. When we gathered around Paul, he was speaking fluent Spanish, and he was telling the young girl about Jesus.

In the same moment, I was mad at Paul for being so weird about knowing Spanish but totally thankful that he reserved his knowledge and used what he knew at the right time. For whatever reason, he felt more comfortable using Spanish when he needed it. And through his willingness to use it, the young lady accepted Christ.

What an example, huh? Is it worth it? Yeah. It's okay to wait until you feel comfortable. It's okay to wait until you uncover someone whom you know will be willing to listen. It's okay to tell someone you've never met, and it's okay to tell someone you've known forever.

Is it worth it? Sometimes more worth it than you realize.

Once there was a guy who would have fallen through the "worth it" cracks. He probably looked like a waste of time. No one expected that he'd do anything with his life. He was dyslexic and had ADHD. He almost failed out of high school. He came from a broken home. His low self-esteem, his low GPA, and his lack of motivation helped just about everyone around him feel like he was destined to meander through life, working some low-paying job and slowly sinning his way out of existence. Even with his dim outlook, some of his friends never gave up on him. Some prayed for him, while others talked to him and tried to help him understand God's love. Most of his friends just had patience.

They loved him enough to invite him to go to church now and then. Their invitations got him to go, and one time the church put him on their mailing list. Since he was on their mailing list, the young man got a summer letter from a youth pastor inviting him to hang out. And they did. Slowly, the misguided, angry teenage boy gave his life over to Jesus.

Talk to the youth pastor who led him to Christ, and he'll tell you that he considers that summer the young man accepted Jesus to be the most disappointing summer ministry he'd ever had. Not much happened. Just one young teenager accepted Jesus. Just one.

I was that young man. I was misdirected, and I remember feeling so alone. I still remember being annoyed with my friends asking me to go to church. I can still remember the hours I logged jogging with my friends and listening to our new youth pastor talking about God. I'll never forget how good it felt to finally know that I was totally and completely loved.

Right now your unsaved friends need to know that unconditional love. They're lost, meandering, alone, and their futures are in question. Your invitation begins the change in their lives. You, reaching into their lives simply by asking them to hang out could change their futures for all eternity.

You. It really is up to you. Yeah, God could do it without you if He wanted . . . but He doesn't. Yeah, someone else might tell them . . . or maybe not. Sure, it's scary. You bet; it's not the easiest thing you'll ever do.

But even with your fear, uncertainty, and unpreparedness, God is calling you. He's begging you to reach out for the sake of your friends. He's calling you to get going. He asking you to get to work.

So do it.

As you share Jesus with your friends, it's my prayer that you'll be willing to be stretched. That you'll shed your fear and embrace God. With your arms fully around Him, your efforts won't return void, and your friends will be eternally affected.

God bless you as you tell your friends about Jesus.

Support the DATA Agenda!

We at Transit support the work of the DATA organization in Africa. Every day more than 5,500 people die from the AIDS virus. And every day more than 1,700 children are infected with HIV. Six times more girls than boys are infected. We cannot stand by while this holocaust happens before our eyes without doing anything to help. This is the moment in history where we will face our humanity, our faith, and our commitment to God. We are commanded to love our neighbor. Africa is our neighbor. Will you help?

Write a letter to the president and your representatives today! You could change the world.

Log on to www.datadata.org today!